from the
BOULEVARD
to the
HIGH ROAD

Larry Phillips

D1571040

Author's Note: This book is a memoir. It reflects the author's present recollections of experiences over time. Some names and characteristics have been changed, some events have been compressed, and some dialogue has been recreated.

Book Layout: Linda Hurley, www.impressionsbookdesignservices.com
Cover Design: Robert Hurley, www.impressionsbookdesignservices.com

From the Boulevard to the High Road/ Larry Phillips. -- 1st ed.
ISBN 9798454695798

Acknowledgments

To those with whom I share an indescribable bond.
My siblings, family, extended family, mentors, and the
late Joe Cox. You are the ones I go to any length to
support, with whom I can disagree strongly while
loving deeply. You changed my life by just being in it.
My connections with you defy the limitations of
distance, time, pen, and ink.

I am what I am

Larry Phillips

Dedication

To my loving wife, Veronica.
The encouraging voice in all my endeavors,
who sacrificed an enormous amount of our time together
for the completion of this work.

Prologue

Hans, a fellow chauffeur and drinking buddy of my father, had immigrated from Germany. It was Hans' habit as he entered the local bar to say hello to each person there. Each one received their own personal greeting "hello, hello, hello, hello…" One day at his usual watering hole, Hans decided it would be easier just to say hello followed by "couple a times." That started a tradition for Hans, my dad, me, and my two sons. It became our greeting to each other, wherever the "proverbial bar stool" happened to be. It could be at the kitchen table or on a plane? Or maybe at Starbucks. So, my greeting to all of you, "couple a times."

This is not a literary masterpiece. I am not a sentence acrobat here to dazzle you with my syntactic dexterity. I am simply the guy next door who writes the way he speaks, directly and from the heart. I am sharing some of my life, for better or worse, my perspective, observations, intense moments, and intimate musings. Exposing some of my vulnerabilities along the way.

Growing up, searching for independence is no walk in the park. When we outgrow our early relations with our parents and siblings, we become accountable for our actions. Navigating life is incredibly challenging, bringing conflict and consequences we can neither ignore nor explain away. My teen years found me charging blindly into the real world armed with racial prejudice, bias, ambition, insecurity, and hormones running wild. I soon found that we live in a deeply colorful and complex world and that I did not know it all.

What I did know, for sure, was that I had to get out of Ozone Park. I was convinced that Lawrence Anthony Phillips was destined for bigger and better things than delivering groceries, washing cars, or working for others. And, despite my love for racehorses, there was no future for me at Aqueduct.

Ah! Now this is the vessel I've been hoping to find.
I'll mend it and use it and make it mine.
I need not the vessel with pride of itself,
Nor one that is narrow to sit on the shelf.

Nor one that is big-mouthed and shallow and loud,
Nor one that displays his contents so proud,
Nor one who thinks he can do things just right.
But this plain vessel filled with power and might.

Then gently He "lifted up" the vessel of clay.
Mended and cleansed it and filled it that day:
He let the vessel know – "There's much work to do…
You are to pour out to others, as I pour into you."

— "The Vessel" by Beulah V. Cornwall

1. My Block

"Don't go in the street, don't even put one foot off the curb," Mom said sternly.

"Yes, Mother," but even then, at the age of five, I had the adventurous spirit to defy boundaries.

Ozone Park, Queens, New York; Rockaway Boulevard, to be exact, was my world. Curb to curb, where I lived, where things happened. "The Boulevard," as we called it, was the lifeline thoroughfare that ran from Brooklyn, through Queens, to Nassau County, Long Island. For the most part, it was retail and commercial, with middle-class single-family homes and apartments above retail establishments.

Our apartment was between 118th Street and 119th Street (Lefferts Boulevard). Where Lefferts and Rockaway intersected was the transfer point for two bus routes, the Q7 and Q10. We lived in an apartment over the Brooklyn Union Gas Company. The three rooms housed all eight of us: my parents, Florence and Richard, my four sisters, Marilyn, Grace, Joan, and Claudia, and my older brother Paul.

On the other side of the gas company was the Farrell Movie Theater. Mr. Nielsen was the manager, and Millie, the matron, was a short lady whose appearance matched her title. She had long, braided hair which she wore crossed over the top of her head like a black tiara. The theater had 38 rows divided by two aisles. The two outside sections had five seats each with a section for children. The left side was for smoking, with little ashtrays attached to the seat backs. The rest was for adults and families. The popcorn machine was my favorite. You could open a small bag, place it on the chute, insert a dime and it dispensed an exact measure of popcorn. It had a plastic bubble on top with a light bulb that gave the illusion that it was freshly popped rather than pre-popped at another location and delivered weekly in large brown paper bags. I often stood under the marquee pressing my face against the glass lobby doors where I could see the popcorn machine. alongside the large, flat, circular tin can where movie films were both delivered and stored for return.

A few steps west of the Farrell was a small gift and card store. Mr. Mailman, the owner, was a tall, slender man with a narrow well-trimmed mustache. He always wore a suit and tie. His inventory of greeting cards, stationery, and postage stamps was a convenience for the neighborhood. My occasional visits almost always resulted in a piece of candy.

Next came the German deli run by Mr. and Mrs. Schroeder. He was a stout man with a round face, and his ruddy complexion was in sharp contrast to his white shirt and apron. The aroma of cinnamon-garnished rice pudding topped with toasted white clouds of meringue clashed with the sharpness of vinegar from the pickle barrel. The Schroeders allowed us to pay "on account." I would give him a note from Mom and, in return, he would give me a bag of groceries and a quart of beer. With no money changing hands until payday.

The appliance and TV repair shop sat between the deli and Dominic's Pizzeria. Joe, the owner, would let me wash out the secondhand refrigerators and appliances. As I got older, he expanded my duties to testing TV tubes for his customers. Each tube had an assigned number, which I would look up and then fit the prongs at the bottom of the tube into the right holes in the electronic testing station. Then I would throw the switch and the tester would show whether the tube was good or bad. I was always thrilled when I could do something with the TV tubes, certainly, it was better and more rewarding than washing out old, mildewed refrigerators. I enjoyed working with Joe. There was always a TV on in the storefront window with antennas wrapped in aluminum foil to assure better reception.

Dominic was a short, heavyset man with an olive complexion and an exceedingly high forehead. By 10 a.m. each day, the pleasant scent of pizza dough wafted a half-block away announcing that lunch was ready. Generally, he was a nice man except when the kids in the neighborhood annoyed him. Then he would pretend to be angry and come running after us with a large knife. I am sure he would not have cut us, but he did a good job of scaring us.

The last store on the block was the Imperial Dry Cleaners. It was run by the Haley family: mother, daughter, and three boys, who lived in the apartment behind the store.

It was several years before I was able to cross the busy Boulevard. But even confined to my side of the street, I still had access to the candy store and the real estate office, where sometimes I would deliver the rent payment: $34.64, late, more often than not.

Within a few blocks, we had access to everything needed to support life: butcher, baker, deli, drugstore, and the Arrow Diner. The prewar dining car was later converted to a chrome diner with a large flashing arrow on its roof. Its parking lot butted up against Sid's gas station, attached to the Castle Inn, an old three-story roadhouse with turrets and parapets. Sid's had once been the carriage house.

Gradually, I was trusted to cross the side streets and explore the neighborhood which was my world in the late 40s and early 50s.

2. The Family

My father was six-foot-tall, slender built, with an orthopedic shoe elevated 6 inches under one foot, the result of infantile paralysis (later known as polio). He presented an imposing figure in his chauffeurs' uniform of black suit and cap, which both hid his baldness and completed the ensemble for driving a stretch limousine for the super-rich in the city of Manhattan, a bus and subway ride away. Dad fought the midtown traffic day and night. But at the end of his workday, and after a few shots of Four Roses rye whiskey, he joined thousands of other working-class stiffs making his way home. He deposited his token in the turnstile and returned to our three rooms and his family. We gathered at the kitchen table every night, many times without my father because of his hours and the commute.

Mom's uniform was a house dress; most times adorned with traces of condiments, cooking grease, dishwater, baby vomit, and a string of safety pins that hung over her left breast like campaign ribbons or sharpshooter metals. The apartment was always clean. My mother washed the windows every week, inside and out. The floors were done on her hands and knees. But when she went out, she was smartly dressed and carried herself proudly like she owned the block, even when they could not even pay the rent.

My sister, Marilyn, ten years older than me, was a tall, thin, blond with long hair. She was smart, bringing home medals and awards in high school, making Mom and Dad proud.

Grace was 2 years younger than Marilyn and equally smart. Shorter, with dark hair and somewhat chunky, Grace played the violin in the school orchestra, worked in the candy store, and saved enough money to buy me my first bicycle. That was a Christmas present and had to last three years. There would be no other gifts from Grace as she moved into nursing school, working toward her R.N.

Joan, the third in a foursome of good-looking girls, had a burning desire to be a ballerina. But along came Tom and she danced into his arms instead.

Brother Paul, four years my senior was sharp rather than intellectual. He had a keen interest in weightlifting and preferred the commercial school rather than John Adams, where the girls had attended and created a legacy.

Claudia came last, happy to say for my mother's sake. She was six years younger than me. So, by the time she started school, I was 12 and well on my way to being a street-smart kid with an adventurous spirit.

***

The three rooms we called home were situated in the rear apartment above the gas company, a storefront where people went to pay their utility bills. The space behind the gas company was leased out to Bushman Plumbing. Mr. Bushman parked his truck in the rear of the building which we called the "yard," beyond which was another fenced lot full of construction equipment.

Our "yard" was devoid of any vegetation, including grass, and had a surface of compacted, crushed stone and ash from the coal furnace. But it was my playground and Mom could see or hear me any time if need be.

The entry foyer had a solid door with no lock, so it was always open. It also served as a shelter for anyone waiting for the Q-7 bus which stopped just across the sidewalk. The second door had a knob that would at least hold the door closed, except when the wind blew. Then the door would blow open and the foyer became a wind tunnel that rattled the frosted glass in the top half of the apartment doors. The walls were lined with brown Congoleum sheet vinyl and there was a handrail on the wall that ran up to the short hall leading to both apartments.

Mrs. Farrell and her two daughters occupied the front apartment. Many days I would race up the 16 steps, two at a time, inhaling the aromas. Knowing there would be a snack or even a whole cake waiting for me.

Our apartment consisted of three rooms, not three bedrooms, just three rooms total. It was not big, my guess would be about 460 square feet. And being number five of six kids raised in those rooms, I can attest we were close. The kitchen had two white porcelain sinks, one shallow and one deep, with the plumbing visible underneath. The deep one was used for bathing young children and doing the laundry. The laundry would then be hung on a line that ran diagonally from the living room/bedroom window to the roof of the Farrell. A small GE refrigerator with the compressor on top held just two ice cube trays, no room for more. Meals were always served on the chrome and Formica table which would be pulled out to the center of the room so that it could accommodate all eight of us. For years, there was a high-chair in the corner.

One door led to the bedroom where there were two beds, a full and a twin, each pushed to the walls creating an aisle for access to the window and the fire escape. Today, I enjoy getting a reaction when I divulge that I slept with my sisters. A single chest and the closet held the clothing and footwear for all of us. When Marilyn married Lewis Groner and Grace went to nursing school, the crush in the closet and the one chest of drawers thinned out.

My father never had more than two suits; one at the dry cleaners and the other on his back. His one pair of orthopedic shoes would be worn until they couldn't be repaired anymore.

The living room always had a convertible sofa and a crib. Our entertainment center was an old free-standing radio. Each night after dinner and homework we would gather in front of the radio listening to programs like the "Lone Ranger," "Inner Sanctum" and "Ozzie and Harriet." We would watch the radio as the characters came to life in our minds.

The air shaft, which served as "Mom's veranda," connected the four adjoining apartments at the kitchen windows. The shaft was open to the roof and only accessible by climbing through the window onto the tar paper surface. There you could experience the mingled aromas of our neighbors' cooking, listen in on their conversations of everyday life and the latest gossip, and of course, borrow the proverbial cup of sugar that was always an arm's length away. The Bowers, a diagonal line of sight from us, engaged in a screaming match every day at dinner time. Without a word, Mom would gently shut the window, shielding us from the occasional profanity, and return to cooking on the four-legged porcelain gas stove.

***

It was a short trip to Grandma's house! My father's mother, Mama Griffin, and her second husband, Poppa George, lived so close I could walk there without crossing any streets. Mama was a robust woman of Swedish descent, always in a housecoat and apron, and was famous for baking, especially crumb cake (still my favorite). Poppa George was a retired policeman who saw the good in everyone and took pride in the fact he only made one arrest in twenty years. Living with them was my father's sister, Aunt Grace, and two boys from the New York Foundling Home, Buster and Tommy. Daddy's other sister, Lillian, married Edgar and they lived in the house across the street with their three children, Eileen, Lillian, and Eddie. Further down 118th Street lived Aunt Gertrude and Uncle Stanley. My strongest and only memory of them is Ritz crackers, they always gave me Ritz crackers. I enjoyed visiting these homes. They had nice things, fully furnished living and dining rooms, and personal bedrooms with wall-to-wall carpet. Even Ritz crackers and crumb cake made me feel special. Later I would learn that my notion of special was "second class."

Visiting my mother's side of the family involved a trip to the Bronx. My Mom and her sisters Edna, Marion, and Agnes or (Sweety) were issues of John Joseph and Mary Frances Campbell. Aunt Marion and Uncle Frank lived in Greenpoint Queens, with daughter Marion, son Frank Junior, and Jack. Visiting them was always an excursion that included bus, subway, and trolley car rides. Our excursions on public transportation became a proving ground for my mother's force-feeding of manners. She was a stickler for all the proper things a gentleman does, hold doors, never be seated if a woman is standing, disembark a bus, and then help women off. These were the days when men wore hats and tipped them to women. The trolley was my favorite, guided by tracks implanted in the street and powered by overhead lines. Sweety and Ray Riley gave birth to Graham. Of course, my cousins, Frank and Jack, nicknamed him "Crackers" (Graham Crackers) which infuriated both mother and child. Everyone but his parents knew he was a spoiled brat and a mama's boy.

Aunt Edna was frail and quite sickly. Her husband, Jim, was a tall, strappy Englishman, with a chiseled chin under a very crooked nose. In hindsight, I guess it had been broken several times. It was alleged that Uncle Jim's drinking drew out his abusive personality both physically and sexually. Those visits brought me in touch with my cousins Loretta, Eileen, and Veronica. Because of uncle Jim's prejudice toward the influx of Puerto

Rican families, we were restricted to the front stoop and warned not to go one step further. Living with Uncle Jim was tumultuous for that whole family. All in all, my cousins were normal and healthy, except for Veronica. She was God awful skinny, with straight platinum hair, and always looked undernourished.

3. School

Back then there was no kindergarten or preschool. You were six years old and went to first grade, that was it. Our Lady of Perpetual Help (OLPH) Catholic School was a two-story red brick building that housed approximately 700 children. The recess area was concrete, surrounded by what seemed to be a 10-foot-high chain-link fence. Once you were in, the gate was closed. It was like going to jail. The yard was where you assembled and exercised which was the best part of the day. Ozone Park was a predominantly Catholic neighborhood. I assumed everyone was Catholic because at school I was told there was no other religion. The school was staffed by Dominican nuns and in 8 years I remember only one who was loving, kind, and understanding. The rest seemed like prison guards. In my memory they were white-faced, fanatical women in black habits with rosaries and copper crosses whom you could never escape. They stood guard at the 9 o'clock mass with World War II clicking frogs that signaled every orchestrated move. They each had their post in the aisle, front, center, and back. Fidget or squirm around and you would get the evil eye from the nearby sentry. I still remember the smell of incense and the twinkling of candles in the red shot glasses. There were mini holy water bowls for finger dipping and blessing yourself. I'm sure they told me why, but I only did it out of fear of chastisement and blind obedience.

Their warden was Mother Beringar. Sister Catherine Edward was notorious for having a disobedient child, or someone with the wrong answer, "assume the angle." The angle was formed by bending over and touching your ankles. She then whacked you across your butt with a half-inch diameter dowel she used as a pointer. The day I had to assume the angle, it hurt so bad I left the building crying and ran home to my mother. When she saw the welt on my backside, she immediately threw her coat on over her house dress and dragged me back to school and into the principal's office. There she pulled down my pants, displaying my battle wounds to Mother Beringar. She declared that if anyone was going to beat Mrs. Phillips' little boy, it would be Mrs. Phillips.

***

I was a blond-haired, blue-eyed, skinny kid with glasses. Dressed in a white shirt with suspenders, I was the perfect picture of a nerd minus the pocket protector. Being the shortest in the class put me first in every line but last picked for the spelling bee. If there was an award for wetting your pants, I was a front runner. It was torture to be told not to raise your hand again when you desperately needed to pee. I must have been a terrible disappointment following my four siblings.

This slow learner survived the eight years with the prison guards along with Mrs. O' Rourke for art and old lady Finnegan for music. On one occasion, Mrs. Finnigan was picking individual students to sing solos. When she got to me, she made me sing several times until she finally gave up and said, "With that voice, you belong in the basement." That humiliation guaranteed that I would never sing in public, not even in the shower.

I can only imagine the harm done to students like myself, by overzealous disciplinarians using fear as a teaching tool and having no thought of a hug for a child who might be scared to death or working through undisclosed problems at home.

For most of my life, I was very bitter at both the Catholic Church and the school system. Nuns were merely young girls who wound up in a convent due to generations of family religious history and were convinced that God had called them. They had little or no life experience.

Despite my struggle and the issues with the nuns, somehow, they pushed me through the eighth grade. I graduated and went on to John Adams High School. Initially, I found the freshman classes easy, then backed off and did not try very hard. Algebra was a killer. I had a tough time with that, and soon found I was not keeping up with my classmates. My grades were failing, and I begged my parents to sign me out. In their wisdom, they realized all the smart genes went to the girls. High school is now just a faint memory.

In those days, a high school diploma was a big deal and provided you a leg up to employment that did not involve getting your hands dirty. It looked as though settling into the working class was going to be my future, unless I could find someone with their foot already in the door.

4. Escape from Ozone Park

Ours was not the only large family in the neighborhood. Around the corner, on the other side of 118th Street, the Cox family, more affectionately called Cox's army, was encamped. The army consisted of seven boys, two girls, and their mother, Ethel. There was no Mr. Cox, at least not in my lifetime. I'm not sure if anyone knew the story behind the missing Mr. Cox, only the consequences of his absence. Mrs. Cox worked days as a domestic and nights restoring the house to order. There was little structure and even less discipline. The two-story house was sometimes a playground, sometimes a battlefield. The basement proved to be perfect for BB gun fights.

Dennis and Joseph were the youngest of the boys. The former was a year older than me and the latter a year younger. Dennis and I became good friends, perhaps because we were both hustlers. We would do anything to make a buck: wash cars, deliver orders, run errands, and rake leaves. We liked the idea of having a dollar in our pocket, even if it was four quarters. Like most 15-year-olds with a few dollars, we talked about venturing off someplace; any place outside of Ozone Park.

Billy Cox came fourth in the pecking order and escaped by joining the Navy. Stationed at Norfolk, Virginia, he abetted us by offering to let us stay at his home off-base. Thinking this was a great idea, in effect running away, we began to plan. Dennis had some money and was willing to share it with me when mine ran out. So, off we went to the port authority bus station in New York City. The trip to Norfolk would take eight hours so we picked up some food for the ride. One dozen Dunkin Donuts was thought to be enough.

However, before going to the ticket window, I thought it would be nice if I called my mother so she would not worry.

"Hi, Mom. Dennis and I are going away to Norfolk, Virginia."

"That's okay. Do you have enough money? Are you dressed warmly?"

"Yes, my flannel-lined jeans, leather jacket, and knit hat."

"Okay, what about Dennis?" I went ahead to give a perfect description of both of us to include the glazed donuts.

Approximately thirteen minutes later, a nicely dressed gentleman called me by name. "Lawrence, and you must be Dennis Cox." This nice gentleman happened to be a port authority detective. So much for my first escape from Ozone Park.

***

Joe Cox was the last born of the nine and seemed to be the most affected by the lack of discipline and even less love. Many of the neighborhood elders saw him as a ragamuffin. His skinny frame barely supported his large mop of blonde, curly hair, giving him the appearance of a pom-pom on a stick. His innocent light blue eyes and deceiving, sorrowful appearance, enhanced his skills.

Evading the truant officer became an art, finding the homemaker who made the best cookies, and boosting a bottle from the milk box was common practice. Raiding the bakery bags of bagels and bread were all part of his early morning activities. All this seemed to be basic training for what was to come as a preteen.

Joe worked hard for whatever he needed and even harder for what he wanted. Soon he wanted more and more. Unable to read or write, he resorted to hawking newspapers and shining shoes in gin mills. Not the best environment for a young boy. Before long, a pedophile presented himself with a pat here and a pat there.

Cigarettes were cool, funny cigarettes were even cooler. Soon he was sniffing, snorting, shooting, popping, and mainlining. Doing anything to catch that ever-elusive high. Like most junkies, he could talk you out of your eye teeth. Selling things that never existed, leaving you waiting for a great deal on a new TV or stereo. After an hour or so, you realized you were scammed and joined the small army of people who longed to break his legs.

***

Mr. Gilbert was a professional thoroughbred horse trainer at Aqueduct Racetrack who seasonally rented a room at the Castle Inn and became a friend of my father. The two of them arranged that I would rise early one day and join Mr. Gilbert for a day at the stables. I was so excited that I was an hour early for my meeting. With the sun barely visible, I joined Mr. Gilbert as he drove to the south end of the stable area. I was introduced to a few horses whose names I do not remember. I do remember, that when we opened the top half of the stall door, the horse came to greet me. At least, that was what I initially thought, but I soon learned he was just looking for breakfast. Mr. Gilbert taught me how to place sugar cubes or carrots in the palm of my hand so as not to be bitten when feeding my new friends. Before long, the barn became populated with exercise boys, hot walkers, and grooms who were all attending to the welfare of the animals. By noontime, I had absorbed the sights, sounds, and aromas that are peculiar to a horse stable. This had been a one-time arrangement between my father and Mr. Gilbert, but I knew I wanted more.

Down Rockaway Boulevard, in descending order, are 118th Street to 114th Street, then the Aqueduct Racetrack. "The Track" as it was known, is situated from 112th to 107th Streets and south to Sunrise Highway. The main entrance is on the Boulevard and was manned by Pinkerton who had the overall security duty for the track. One of their challenges was to deny entrance to juveniles like myself. The hole in the chain-link fence, a hundred yards from the Boulevard, was my normal point of access. Soon I was able to spot the "pinkie patrol" and knew where and how to duck out of sight.

It was during my early teens that I met Suzanne Zinser, while still a young lady, she was a woman to someone my age. She garnered great respect as one of the first three women licensed to be a professional thoroughbred racehorse trainer.

She had a three-year-old mare, Mammy Pleasant, who was kind of docile, not full of fire like some of the two-year-olds. Suzanne let me clean the tack and taught me the art of mucking out the stalls. This involved removing only the manure and soiled straw, saving the dry straw to be reused. Grooming was a daily routine after a workout. Mammy had to be walked, cooled down, and washed. Many times, I was trusted to do some of that. When summer ended, I continued to get up early, showing up at the stables and working until I had to go to school. I had great aspirations of becoming a jockey; since I was short, light, and had a great love of the animal. Oh, yeah, and naive. Did I mention naive?

One morning, before Mammy Pleasant was due to race in the afternoon, she received a visit from a veterinarian who gave her a shot. Being a young, savvy "man about the stables," I assumed it was a hotshot to make her win. Once again, did I mention naive? I went home and told everyone: mother, father, aunts, uncles; anyone with two dollars to spare. Two hours before post time I showed Suzanne my half-page betting slip; winking and assuring her that her secret was safe with me. To this day, I am still not sure whether she thought it was cute or that I was getting into the dark side of the sport. She had a serious conversation with me, and I never took another bet, not ever. It turned out the shot had been precautionary for a simple cold.

That afternoon, like most of my summer afternoons, I had watched the race from the backside of the track opposite the grandstands where the starting gate was loaded. Taking in the sunshine, the sights, the sounds, and the myriad of fragrances (tractor fumes, horse manure, and hot dogs). They are still vivid in my memory. Uppermost, though, is the voice of Freddie Cappercella, the track announcer. A voice so distinctive I mimicked him for years. First was "The horrrrses are on the track!" and the crowd would move forward to a vantage spot at the rail. As soon as the outriders and gatekeepers loaded the horses in their proper position, Freddy would command, "It is nowww post time." Suddenly, with the sound of a bell, "And they're off." The thunder of hoof beats filled the air. The slapping, clapping, and cheering of the racing fans and the track people blended to produce an overwhelming sensation. After as many as eight races, I would go home hungry and full of stories of the day. Eddie Arcaro won three races or Sunny Jim Fitzsimmons was on the backstretch. Sunny Jim was a one-time jockey turned trainer with seven Triple Crown contenders, including Nashua.

My life on the track did not last more than a few years, but it kept me off the streets where some of my friends had been playing with zip guns, funny cigarettes, dice, beer, and booze. To this day, I love to stand and gaze at those magnificent animals. And, by the way, Mammy Pleasant never did win a race.

***

My sister Grace and Bob McGarvey were married soon after Grace graduated from nursing school and Bob was discharged from the Air Force. Twelve months later they started a family. It was thanks to Bob, and his father, a New York City detective on the Juvenile Aid Bureau, that I avoided getting into a jam when I was pinched for gambling in public.

As I passed Woolworths on Liberty Avenue, I took small side-steps and peered through the large window at the displays. I came to a sudden stop when, right next to a game of Monopoly, I noticed a shiny box. On its top was a picture, in the foreground a roulette wheel, the green table cover laid out in rectangles of colored numbers. The background showed a group of well-dressed people, obviously anxious to place their bets. It seemed to be calling to me. Here was an opportunity to make some easy money. After all, even at my tender age, I knew the house never loses. It was a minimal investment that would bring in extra income. The next day I set up shop on the back stoop of the Castle Inn. Before long, the police arrived to break up my new enterprise. Apparently, the line-of-sight neighbors took exception to the small gathering of teenage boys passing money back and forth. My juvenile delinquency card read, "Gambling in the street for money."

When I grew tired of our cramped family quarters, Bob once again stepped in, offering me the couch in their small basement apartment. He also set me up with a friend of his who had a book edge gilding business in Manhattan. I tried my hand at putting gilt edges on bibles, but it didn't last long.

Next, I went to my other brother-in-law, Louis Groner, who was married to my oldest sister, Marilyn. Louie was a big man, not fat, but bulky with strong hairy hands that extended through the ends of his signature leather jacket. He looked like a modern-day biker. He had no motorcycles but was a big fan of nice cars, especially Plymouths and Chryslers, and was willing to work extra hours to maintain them.

He worked days at the Jamaica Bus Company and pumped gas nights and weekends at Sid's Gas Station. Those were the days when someone pumped your gas, checked your oil, and cleaned your windshield. Payments were made in cash, and it was customary to tip the gas jockey. Louie's ability to work the pumps and the people was evident in his tip jar. He used his influence to find me a job at the bus company. I worked nights, sweeping and cleaning out buses. Being a young man lacking in work ethic and more interested in masturbating several times a day, I had little energy or inclination to do a good job. Nevertheless, Louie was instrumental in my getting my next job, installing seat covers and convertible tops at an auto interior shop. That one did not last long either.

***

On the north side of the Boulevard, between 118th and 117th Streets was Memorial Park. The triangular-shaped park had red brick inlays around the flagpole. The circumference was a sidewalk with concrete park benches with wooden seating areas convenient for carving initials. The outer ring had boxed planters protecting the base and root system of the shade trees. This park became the gathering place for the "Boulevard Boys."

Hanging out there one day, Frankie Klinski bragged of his association with Joyce Ambrose, a neighborhood girl known to be "accommodating." He claimed he could set up a meeting with her. Two days later, game on. She was going to meet us at Glenn

Morris, the construction dumping ground behind Johnny Blades Feed and Fertilizer. And the promise was that she was going to show us a good time.

It was a hot, muggy, summer night. The bales of fresh-cut hay were conveniently stacked against the back wall of the warehouse and provided a comfortable spot for our promised adventures. My pulse increased as a female silhouette appeared from the darkness, *could this be my first encounter beyond kissing and petting?* Feeling the excitement mounting, I fumbled through my limited repertoire of romantic advances until she either became legitimately frightened or thought she would be funny by screaming "Rape!" Her squeal alerted some neighbors who were sitting out on their front stoop, and they called the police. Frankie and I decided to take off, leaving Joyce fully clothed and unmolested.

As the evening progressed, Frankie and I became aware that our friends were being stopped and questioned by the police, who were obviously and actively looking for us. Eventually, we decided it would be best to turn ourselves in before one of them got arrested for the marijuana we knew they were carrying.

In our minds, we had not done anything. So, we hastened through the streets toward the 106th Precinct, trying to avoid being detected by the police before we got to the station house. We sheepishly approached the Desk Sargent, "Sir, I think someone may be looking for us." He directed us upstairs to the detective squad. Two tall, gray-haired "suits" took names, addresses, and phone numbers. We nervously tried to explain that we had not done anything. "Then why are you here?" I could hardly tell them that we had almost done something.

The two detectives directed us to sit at a table and then left the room. Twitching, turning, and questioning each other as to what we hadn't done, we noticed a .38 revolver sitting on the table in plain view. It was probably empty and left to see how tough or stupid we were.

Our parents had been called. Frank got sent home with his mother because he was under 16 years of age. When my father arrived, I was already in a holding cell. That was the first time I ever heard him use the "F word." He was recovering from hip surgery, and came hobbling in on crutches, swearing he would take his crutch and break it over my "fuck'n back." He wanted to bail me out, but I told him not to bother. He did not have the money and it would only be a few days until I went to court. I could sit it out.

I was the sole occupant of this 8 x 10 cell with two six-foot benches. I sat on one, contemplating my future until I felt as if the walls were shifting closer and a thousand ants were crawling over my skin.

I soon learned that when you have done something wrong, the most horrible thing is to be left alone. Early the next morning, I was transported to the Men's House of Detention on Atlantic Avenue in Brooklyn, along with a half dozen others. Handcuffed one to the other, we were paraded into the reception area, stripped-down, showered, and ordered to "spread our cheeks." After being issued a jumpsuit and slippers, I was suddenly very envious of my buddy. I wasn't comfortable being housed with a bunch of guys who had probably done what I had almost done.

The adolescent block was long, with cells on both the upper and lower level. Mine was on the upper with a narrow walkway overlooking the lower half of the block. The only daylight came through an eight-inch-wide barred window, several floors above the street. After the evening meal, our spoons were collected and counted. The day room was closed and we were ordered to our cells. The gate clinked shut and I was in for the night. The world turned to white clarity as a crack of lightning struck. The sound set off an avalanche of uncontrollable shivers.

On the third day, I was transported to the courthouse in Queens. I was held in a side room until it was my turn. I was walked out in front of the judge and was elated to see my father and my Aunt Grace. The court-appointed attorney offered the police reports to the judge and said, "It seems like the girl is more guilty than the boys, your Honor." Shivering before the judge, he bellowed "A.C.O.D." and banged the gavel. Puzzled, I looked to my father. My lawyer took me by the arm and led me into the marble corridor. He introduced me to my probation officer who explained that A.C.O.D was an acquittal in contemplation of dismissal. Meaning, if I stayed out of trouble and did not get arrested for six months, they would drop the charges and my record would be expunged.

On the way home, while my father was reading me the riot act and Aunt Grace was preaching abstinence and how some of those kinds of girls have diseases, I "yessed" them to death and was as polite as I could be, knowing there would be more preaching from Mom as soon as I walked through the door. After an hour or so things cooled down. I was still mulling over how easy it would be to get in trouble. Back in the day room, I had met some apprentice jailhouse lawyers, one who was sure if you joined the service the judge would discharge your case. All that played over and over in my head. Finally, I called my probation officer and he confirmed it was a possibility.

"When will you be 17?"

"October 9th."

"Let's wait until your birthday, then if you still want to enlist, we'll go to court. Until then, stay out of trouble."

That gave me three months to work on my parents. In mid-October, my probation officer and I petitioned the court, and the case was dismissed. On December 16, 1957, Mom and Dad went with me to Whitehall Street in lower Manhattan. At the military induction center, I was tested, given a physical, and sworn in. We had a short goodbye. I was oblivious to the emotions they were feeling, their delinquent little boy was now Uncle Sam's problem.

As the bus navigated through the downtown streets headed for the Holland Tunnel, a slide show of images clicked in my head: my father's threat with one crutch, the jail cell, Rockaway Boulevard, Ozone Park, the only place I had ever known, and Fort Dix the absolute unknown.

5. You're in the Army Now

The charted bus was slowly and meticulously maneuvered to its resting place. The way a plane is guided at the airport. With a pneumatic wheeze, the brakes and door were activated.

"Okay, dumb asses, unload!" Before I could even see him, I knew he meant business.

"Move it, move it." Then he appeared before me, standing in the aisle, blocking the exit. His appearance and demeanor declared that he was no one to be questioned and I had the feeling we were not going to be buddies.

He bellowed, "Unload! Get off, get off." I was petrified, unable to move past this bald, spit-shined, head-to-toe mass of muscles.

"What's the matter? Do you take exception to being called a dumb ass? Then you must be a smart ass. We like smart asses at Fort Dix."

He stepped aside and I silently and quickly exited; like a cockroach when the lights come on.

The first few days were spent in the intake area. Several busloads of young boys arrived, unknowing and unsuspecting. They shifted and shuffled, with no idea of what they were supposed to do next. Then, suddenly, all focus was on the voice spewing out commands as he grabbed one person after another.

"Stand here and don't move! you're the first. You, over here behind him."

"Yes, sir." came the timid replies as we hurried to obey.

Soon the herd of hairy, shabby, wrinkled, unshaven recruits (and at least one fugitive from justice) had formed our first of many military formations.

"What an unsightly mass of humanity... and I'm not sure about the human part."

So it went on, learning a whole new vocabulary; fall in, right face, left face, and about-face forward march. And march we did. First, to the barbershop with eight manned chairs in a row where we got in and out with lightning speed. The large mirror was just there to humiliate us. At the quartermaster (another new term), I was handed a clipboard with a blank form and directed to proceed to station one. At station one I was measured: 16-inch neck, 26-inch inseam, 32-inch sleeve, etc., etc. At station two I received a duffel bag. I continued through the warehouse, station by station, as I was issued socks, undershorts, uniform shirts, ties, pants, jackets, shoes, boots, and assorted equipment. Stuffing the entire issue into the duffel bag was challenging, made even more difficult by the accompaniment of the screaming staff which served to increase my nervousness.

One recruit dropped a boot and was moving along without it when a corporal got in his face screaming. "This is your boot, are you going to fight a war on one foot?"

"No, Sargent."

"Sargent! I'm a corporal - two stripes. Sargent gets three. Get that straight."

"Yes, Sargent. Uh, uh, Corporal."

The fumbling mass of confused recruits with one hand on their bag, the other rubbing their head, searching for phantom hair. This "orientation" lasted a few more days, followed by basic combat training with weapons of minimal destruction.

***

There was much talk about the 38th parallel, Syngman Rhee, MacArthur, Mao Zedong, and the Chosin Reservoir. I truly did not understand any of it. The Korean War cease-fire was in July

1953, only four years before my enlistment. The training officers, for the most part, were veterans of that conflict. Who better to train the next generation of warriors than those who had seen mass casualties and wholesale frostbite?

January and February in New Jersey supplied frozen ground and, for good measure, the night fire range was watered to make it more realistic. The icicles hung from the barbed wire as we crawled on our backs, watching the traces racing overhead in the black sky. I was living what I had seen on the Movietone News at the Farrell. Basic training was eight weeks of teamwork and lots of physical training. If a trainee was overweight, he lost it, if he was light in the ass, he put it on.

The days were long and hard. One day on the hand grenade range, Jack Stapleton was having a hard time staying awake. While his torso displayed good muscle definition, that day he did not have the strength to raise his eyelids. The instructor barked. "Having trouble staying awake? Stand up!"

Jack remained in the bleachers and continued nodding off despite my poking him to keep him awake. Suddenly the instructor lunged forward into Jack's face and screamed. "Wake up, hold this." He then placed a grenade in Jack's hand and pulled the pin.

"Fall asleep now! Then see what happens."

Tiny beads of sweat appeared on Jack's face as he squeezed the grenade so tight the tips of his fingers lost their color. The instructor continued to describe the devastating power that Jack held in his hand. The beads transitioned to a stream of water dripping from his chin. For the rest of the class, our attention was split between Jack and the instructor. At the close of the class, the grenade was cautiously removed from Jack's death grip and tossed aside only to sizzle and pop like a firecracker. There was a collective exhale of stale breath.

If there was anything my mother had not taught me about discipline manners and respect, I learned it in my eight weeks at Fort Dix. Upon completion of basic, I was physically strong, mentally alert, and morally... well, maybe not morally straight.

I received orders for pole lineman training at the Communication School at Fort Gordon, Georgia. This involved several hours of training in the "Pole Orchard" every day. Braces with gaffs were strapped to our legs. As we used them to climb the giant timbers, we would ascend a few steps, slide to the ground, ascend a few steps, and slide to the ground again. Sliding down incorrectly resulted in sharp splinters embedded in our legs. A life-changing lesson was learned the day a student slid down from the top with bent knees, hugging the pole until he reached the earth below. Wooden slivers in his legs were the least of his problems, several had pierced his testicles. That did it! None of us slipped down the pole after that.

Payday brought us $78 a month and a weekend pass. I made my first visit to the town of Augusta and checked into the Augusta Hotel. It was a shabby little place, basically a storefront with an upstairs, and not too many rooms. Being the smart-ass that I was, I asked the clerk if there was room service. He translated that to mean that I was looking for female companionship for the night. A short time later I answered a knock at my door to find a woman old enough to be my mother. She invited herself into my room and what happened that afternoon happened very quickly. I never got her name, but she got mine. *Stupid.* I sure was growing up fast.

***

I now had a military occupation specialty (MOS) and was reassigned to Kaiserslautern, Germany. This baby faced, not yet 18-year-old, was in a foreign country without foreign language training. Awestruck, I observed in silence, the remnants of the war from a decade and a half before. I could not help but observe and compare, quickly becoming aware of the privileged lifestyle we enjoyed in the States.

My first venture off the base was with a fellow soldier, Jimmy Johnson, a tree topping lumber jack from Oregon. He was a nice man, but a long way from attractive. His teeth were crooked, with an overbite that caused him to salivate. He offered to take me downtown and show me where the guesthouses were and how to order a beer. That sounded good to me, so off we went.

It was a sunny Saturday afternoon and as our eyes transitioned from bright daylight to the dark beer hall. Jimmy showed me how to remove the ceramic cap over the top of the bottle by slapping it with my finger. I tried several times with no success. Then I gave up and used both hands to open mine and started to drink. I enjoyed both the flavor and the atmosphere. We made our way to another guest house across the street. Carefully navigating the cobblestones, I realized that one beer had made me a bit light-headed. German beer was stronger than any I ever drank. Jim was having a great time at my expense. By the time I finished the second beer, I was drunk. He decided I had had enough and put me on the streetcar back to the post.

After several trips downtown, I learned that the Augusta was not the only place that had middle-aged women eager to relieve young men of their discretionary income. Kaiserslautern had a community called "Ten Mark Alley." There for ten marks ($2.50), you could throw discretion to the wind. It would be fair to say that sometimes I exercised too little discretion in a town with too much wind.

***

The downside of being 17 with no drinking experience was that after a few episodes you tend to think, *I've got this.*

While on maneuvers in the countryside, Sgt. Odem informed us of a guesthouse not far away.

"Just across the clearing, in plain sight from the end of the camp road, about a five-minute walk. Take all your gear. It's a tactical exercise. Watch out for the MPs."

When we arrived, we found it truly was a farmer's home with one room set up as a pub. It had several tables and a well-worn wooden bench that stretched around the walls. Our arrival was a boon to their economy, and we were welcomed graciously.

Even though we knew the establishment was off-limits, we settled in, and the tables soon became cluttered with empty and partially empty bottles. We were roused from our revelry when the innkeeper shouted, "Comrades, the MPs come, MPs come."

He opened a door and motioned us into a dark room. "Go here! Go here!"

All ten of us hurried through the door in absolute silence. The MP s entered to find, in plain sight, cold, wet bottles on the tables but no drinkers. I dared to turn on my flashlight and found my face inches from a cow's ass. When the MPs had gone, we started, a few at a time, to return to camp. When I finished my last beer, I exited, alone, into the dark of night. No problem, I thought. Just draw a line of sight from the guesthouse, across the field to the road, and into the camp. Every few minutes, I looked back to the light from the farmhouse to make sure I was on course. That brought me great comfort until the occupants went to bed and the lights went out. Now drunk, cold, and alone, I was relying on the moonlight reflecting on the snow to guide me back. Shortly, I arrived at the road to the camp. Nope, wrong road. As I backtracked to the clearing in search of a different road, it started to snow. At that point, the barley hops and malt began taking full effect. The only sound was my feet crunching the snow and the volcanic belching from my stomach.

At last, I found some footprints and was sure that if I followed them, they would lead me back to camp. With renewed hope, I started off until I realized they were my tracks from hours earlier. Now tired, drunk, frustrated and still lost, I decided to stay in one spot until the morning light. Gathering a few pine branches, I made a bed in the snow, and went to sleep, or more likely passed out.

I was awakened by the sound of a generator. Hopeful, I followed the sound and realized that camp had only been fifty yards away from my sleeping spot. I quietly stepped into the squad tent and backed up to the heater to thaw out. I had just broken the sheet of ice that had fused the flaps of my pile cap to the turned-up collar on my field jacket, when a muffled voice from inside a sleeping bag said, "Phillips, that heater has been off for hours. You have to hook up the fuel can, to get it started again. And where were you all night?"

***

Not long after I learned to drink beer, I learned to pull guard duty. I was attached to the base security team and posted at the back gate. The orders for that two-man post read, in part, "Stop and check all motor vehicles and foot traffic for proper ID, military and civilian alike." Taxicabs were not allowed on the base. Passengers had to be dropped off at the entry gate and proceed on foot. One night at about 11, a taxi pulled up and four black men got out and started to shuffle around as if to find money to pay their fare. I sensed they were going to stiff the driver and make a run for the gate. I alerted my partner just as they charged the gate. We quickly came to port arms and commanded "HALT!" We detained three of the four, and with them spread eagle against the wall, I summoned the Officer of the Guard. That was the highlight of the night.

Later, after midnight curfew, the MPs from town patrol returned in their radio car and we started to chat. The lights at the guard shack shone down into the front seat of the car, illuminating the two uniformed MPs. When they inquired as to our evening, I began to relate the details of the gatecrashers.

"It was a nice quiet night until four niggers tried to run the gate."

I went on to criticize the "niggers" for their behavior repeating the N-word several times. The conversation ended and the MPs went away, ending their tour.

About 45 minutes later, from inside the gate, we were approached by a black man in civvies with a .45 in his hand. He said that he had been the third MP, in the backseat of the car. "Tell me again about those niggers," he said, ominously.

Now he's screaming and pointing the pistol at my face. I managed to chamber a round in my carbine, and we were locked in each other's sights. His face was black as night, with beads of sweat glistening in the glow of the overhead floodlights.

I screamed, "Put that gun down." The churning in my stomach told me my mouth had gotten my ass in some big trouble.

"No, tell me to my face about the niggers?"

My heart thumped hard against my rib cage, as I zoomed in on his trembling finger. One squeeze could be life-ending for one of us, maybe both. Frightened by the look in his eyes, I forced my dry throat to speak. "Let's put our weapons down and talk about it."

"You want to talk to a nigger!"

I tried to explain. "Not all blacks are ..." as I fumbled over the N-word again. "There's a difference between good colored people and ..."

His nervous finger continued to cradle the trigger.

At that moment, the duty officer brought his Jeep to a screeching halt. With both of us highlighted in the headlights, Lt. Wilson defused the situation. He made it clear that no good could come of this. All parties involved would have to partake in a thorough investigation. Truthfully, none of us wanted that. Reluctant handshakes and daylight ushered in the dawn. My sweat-soaked shorts and T-shirt were a testament to the reality of what had happened.

I realized I had been exposed to a type of ingrained ignorance that I had absorbed as easily as my ABCs. My father used words like gook, Guinea, and nigger. Everyone was painted with one broad stroke. He wasn't the only one that nurtured racism. It was commonplace in my mostly white neighborhood. None of those people had ever done anything to deserve a derogatory title. In retrospect, the episode had taught me a good lesson that changed my thinking and my vocabulary. Thankfully, my time with the security team ended without further incident.

***

I was assigned to temporary duty in the town of Darmstadt. I would spend much of my tour housed in a room with seven men, all of whom hailed from south of the Mason-Dixon line. Initially, I could not stand the country music they played. Soon, I deliberately began a collection of heavy classical music. It was a daily race to the jointly-owned record player to see whose music got on first. This caused mounting friction between us. I was fast and smart and soon they became grumpy and irritated.

One day, several of my roommates insisted that I remove the classical music When I refused, they began to threaten me. Perched on our writing table was a bottle of green fountain pen ink. During this heated exchange, Bobby Jo (or was it Jo Bob?) from Harlan, Kentucky, threatened to knock me down and paint my dick green. Of course, I replied, "You and who else's army?" When the dust settled and the bruises and contusions tended, I carried the green reminder between my legs for about two weeks. The country music grew on me and didn't seem so bad. Imagine that.

When one of the seven was transferred back to the states, he was replaced by Wilhelm Braun, a German American, whose family lived in Eberstadt, the very next town from where we were stationed. We often visited his family, spending pleasant days at his home and experiencing the authentic German lifestyle. It was there, one sunny Sunday afternoon, I learned to drink depth charges. While my tolerance for the German beer had improved, the depth charge was a new challenge. We would place a shot glass of schnapps above the rim of a beer stein, release the shot glass, and drink the contents before it hit the bottom. Uncertain to this day how I returned to the base, I do remember being in some shrubbery with one shoe on. The other never surfaced. I sat on my bunk with one foot on the floor, hoping that it would keep the room from spinning. This was just another learning experience, one not to be repeated. There were many good experiences in my tenure, most of which centered around the pursuit of young ladies.

***

Victor Novelli came up with a few dollars to rent a VW Bug so that we could explore the countryside. It was my responsibility to supply gas money. On one of our weekend escapades, we came upon a village carnival. As we perused the attractions, we happened upon a game of chance. A ring toss was run by two extremely attractive young ladies. The game was housed in a gypsy wagon with the sidewall raised like an awning, displaying the stuffed animals and other prizes. The exterior was painted in bright colors, depicting the German countryside. It was colorful and inviting like something out of a Hollywood movie production. But far more colorful were the two_frauleins. They were dressed in traditional German garb; *dirndl* skirt (pronounced DEERn-dul), *dirndbluse,* a blouse with puffed sleeves, and *dirndlschurze,* an apron. Tradition dictates that when the apron bow is tied on the left, the wearer is single or available; tied on the right means she is either married or spoken for. Both girl's aprons were tied on the left!

Victor and I spent all the money we had to keep the girls engaged in "conversation." That is stretching it a bit, we did not speak German and the girls spoke little English. Allison was blonde with electric blue eyes and a smooth, pearl white complexion. Brandy was a brunette with brown eyes and an alabaster glow.

"One mark, bitte. You play, yes? One mark, bitte." A mark was equal to 25 cents. Victor and I remained for several hours trying to make our marks last. The two girls were part of a gypsy family caravan. They gave us their schedule, so each weekend we could find them in another town with our pockets full of quarters.

With Wilhelm's help, we wrote them letters in German. When we were with them, we used sign language, a German/English dictionary, and the flirtatious language of love, including translating song lyrics. One song was *"I'm Just a Lonely Boy."* I worked exceedingly hard to convince Allison that I was a lonely boy, and she could change that.

One night after the carnival shut down, with an index finger to her lips, motioning me to be silent, Allison snuck me into the room built into the end of the wagon. It had a built-in bunk with an old canvas mattress and some stuffed teddy bears, nothing else. We made love in almost total silence and darkness until Brandy knocked at the door. She signaled me to meet up with Victor where we had parked the car earlier that day.

This went on for a few months. One weekend, Allison and I used the VW while Brandy and Victor used what became known as the bunkhouse. The backseat was ridiculously small but somehow our youth, agility, and passion helped us to overcome this obstacle. I had been told once that if they cracked my head open, they would only find hundreds of little vaginas with wings flying around inside. It was hard to deny that my mindset and personality were being formed around sex and alcohol.

***

My greatest regret was that I did not take advantage of the opportunities to travel around Europe while I was there. I never realized how close I was to Paris and other European sights. I should have paid more attention in geography and history classes. It could have been the birth of a thirst for both education and travel.

***

The cool, crisp night air stung my face as I stepped through the hatch onto the porpoise-gray deck of the USS Derby, a troopship transporting us back to the United States. I was waiting for Dennis Campbell and Larry Miller to join me, so we could plan the trip to our next duty assignment at Fort Lewis, Washington. The three of us served in the 25th Signal Battalion. Campbell was from Boston and Miller lived in Bridgeport, Connecticut. The game plan was to drive across the country in Campbell's 1957 Ford Fairlane convertible. The salty ocean mist dampened our uniforms but not our spirits. We exchanged addresses and phone numbers and agreed to share expenses for what we calculated to be a ten-day trip.

Six days later, we arrived at the Brooklyn Army Terminal. The sight of me getting into the chauffeur-driven, shiny black, stretch limousine surprised the guys. I never gave the impression that I came from money because I did not. My father often used the limousine for personal transportation because we never owned a family car.

When our leave was up a few weeks later, we rallied at the apartment on Rockaway Boulevard and headed out for Fort Lewis. Our first layover was Cleveland where we arrived early enough to find a lakeside park and some girls to hang out with. Just after dark when a newfound acquaintance and I were becoming intimate on a beach blanket when we were interrupted by a deep voice. "Park closes at dusk." I rolled over to see horse hooves wedged into the soft beach sand. The voice belonged to the cop in the saddle.

Days two, three, and four were exhilarating as we accelerated westward, breaking each evening to find lodging and meet more people. None of us had ever seen that part of the country and, for the first time, I understood the lyrics "amber waves of grain."

On a hot July day, we could see snow on the Montana mountains. As we arrived at Glacier National Park, we exited the convertible and had a snowball fight. That afternoon, we drove around the park to St. Mary's Lake and frolicked in the crystalline cryogenic water. Montana gave us an added surprise as we came upon the Blackfoot Indian Reservation where a national Native American pow wow was taking place. Tribes from all over the United States were represented in full traditional dress, feathers, and face paint. The displays of Indian crafts were endless.

As we continued, Mount Rainier, also snow-covered, appeared on the horizon. The setting sun pinkened the glazier, with the summit shimmering into watercolor, and fading into the night sky. Mount Rainier is the backdrop for Seattle and Tacoma. Native Americans first knew it as "Tahoma" (mother of waters). Our destination, Fort Lewis, was on the west side of Mount Rainier.

***

We reported in and settled down. I was fortunate, because of my rank, I was assigned a room at the end of the barracks. It came with a beautiful view of Mount Rainier, quite a change from my room on Rockaway Boulevard.

We took advantage of Dennis and his car to recon the local landscape, searching for hangouts, coffee shops, and beer halls. At top of the list were the USO dances held at the base recreation centers. The girls we met at those dances primarily came from two Tacoma area schools; an elite girl's prep school and a Catholic institution that, of course, preached the virtues of abstinence. I prayed I would find a nonbeliever.

It was at one of those dances that I met Barbara Bauer. She was good-looking, well-endowed, and carried herself like she was looking for an office job and dressed the part. In Queens, I would have called her a snob. She and I hit it off well enough, although I felt somewhat intimidated by her vocabulary and intellect. I tried not to display my lack of schooling, remembering that profanity was a sign of a limited vocabulary. While she had many positive traits, her late-model MG Midget was the deal maker.

As the relationship progressed, we spent several evenings a week tooling about the area in her "motorized skateboard." We shared much of our history and finally hit the benchmark "meet the parents" date. Upon arrival at their residence, two large lawn signs glared out east and west "Nixon." *Now, this would be a challenge.* I had barely heard of Nixon. The last two years I was in Germany, the names I heard most were Johnny Cash, Earnest Tubb, and Hank Williams. *You will get through this; nod, agree, and apologize for not keeping up while out of the country.* Dinner was good and her parents were pleasant. Mr. Bauer offered me an after-dinner drink which I declined; not knowing a cordial from a cognac. While the ladies cleaned up after dinner, he took his drink and motioned me to join him in the den. Taking a seat in the large barrel-winged chair, I felt the air swish out of the thick leather, seat cushion.

"Smoke?" he asked, opening an inlaid wooden cigar box.

"No, thank you. I don't smoke."

"That's good, ever tried?"

"I tried a few times, choked each time, and decided it's not for me."

Mr. B removed the cigar, unwrapped it, cut the end off with special clippers, and moistened the outer leaf with his tongue. He was very methodical with the whole process, holding the match low and away from the end of the stogie, watching the flames draw into the end. A few puffs and that tightly rolled log of tobacco had a red glow on the tip. I took in the ambiance of the room: leather top desk, wall to wall bookcases holding sets of matched books, both hard-covered classics and reference.

"Barbara tells me you'll be discharged at the end of the year."

"Yes, sir, December 15." Suddenly, I thought this might be a job interview or a man-to-man talk about the dangers of violating his little girl. I had been talking to Barb about staying on in Washington and I'm sure she had shared that with her parents. However, that was a lie, everything I told her was a lie. I only told her what I knew she wanted to hear.

After exhaling a long, swirling, pillow of smoke, his forehead creased as he said, "I often go to New York on business."

"Where exactly do you go?" He mentioned Yonkers, Manhattan, and some upstate areas; outlining enough places to make me aware that he knew New York. I suddenly became aware he was sending me a message.

Did I mention Barb was from the elite school and believed strongly in abstaining? I continued the lies with her old man and one lie led to another. Soon everything was a lie. I sat in the privacy of the den telling him how much I thought of his baby and my plans for the new year. I must have been convincing because the rest of the meeting was an exchange of family history and other pleasantries. Nothing of him tearing my heart out should I get out of line with Barbara. My promise was that upon discharge, I would go to New York, visit with my family, return to find a job, and we would get married. The truth was I would fly to New York and she would never hear from me again.

***

The plane taxied to the runway, the thrust pushing me back into my seat. As I looked out the window at the Sea-Tac Airport fading into the distance, somewhere beneath was an attractive young girl in a sports car whose father, if he knew, would want to avenge his little girl's heartbreak.

I am not proud of my behavior; I still feel guilty when I think of it. I was young and thinking with my organ instead of my brain. I hope that she forgave the scum who wore down her resistance with a million little lies and promises.

6. Home Again

On December 16, 1960, my parents were to meet me at Newark Airport. It wasn't long before I realized my flight was running late and we had been circling. After a while, the captain announced, "Ladies and gentlemen, they are very busy at the airport. We are stacked up, but it shouldn't be too much longer. Thanks, folks."

We circled for another hour before we finally landed. My parents met me at the gate. My mother's fevered appearance told me that something was wrong.

"Hi, Mom." She took me into her arms and held me like she did when I was a child. When she released me, tears were glistening on her eyelashes, threatening to drop down her cheeks.

"Mom, what's wrong?"

"We heard rumors of a plane crash."

"I guess that's why we're late."

As we made our way home, snippets came from the car radio. There had been a mid-air collision of two commercial air liners. In the days that followed, details surfaced to include the death of 128 passengers and six persons on the ground. One passenger, an 11-year-old boy, had been tossed from the wreckage, landing in a snowbank. He had been rescued by police and residents. His charred and broken body was transported to a hospital where he succumbed to his injuries the next morning.

One of the flights had been bound for Idlewild Airport (now JFK). The flight path was directly over our apartment. We had been very lucky.

***

I spent the following months doing menial work, primarily as an apprentice in a machine shop. I operated some machines and did grunt work. When summer approached, I worked nights and weekends at Rockaway Playland Amusement Park. I was a carnival barker at the nickel pitch. I was a quick study and had soon mastered my barker schtick. "Step right up, step right up, pitch your nickel, win a prize, only five cents. Step right up, win a prize."

One sweltering Sunday afternoon there was a sizable crowd throwing their money away, and it was my job to keep them playing. Three young ladies were approaching from across the street and I shouted. "Here they are ladies and gentlemen, straight from a three-week engagement in the Lincoln Tunnel where they stopped all traffic, the Lee sisters." The crowd tittered and with that encouragement, I continued.

"Yes, the famed Lee sisters." I went on as they entered the crowd. Now everyone was looking at the three girls and I barked out, "Ug Lee, Home Lee, and Beast Lee."

I did not know it then, but the joke was on me. I soon learned God had a sense of humor and the girls, Flo, Carol, and Stephanie were good sports.

Soon I had a lady of my own. She worked at the refreshment stand and after a few conversations, I learned she was married, unhappy, and horny. One night after work we were parked in a dark, secluded area where the beach grass was taller than the car. We sat, talked, and made love. It was well after midnight when a police car rolled up next to us. The officer was polite as he told us it was not safe. "You should go up to the parking lot; at least you'll have some light. If something happened to you here no one would ever find you."

"Yes sir. Thank you, officer."

The next night, we went back to the very same spot, only to be interrupted again by the very same cop. This time he told us "Don't be so cheap, go get a room."

When Playland closed for the season, my carnival days were over. I hung out in the neighborhood with the guys, occasionally catching up with "The Lees," at Marlow's, a bar on Lefferts Boulevard.

Carol became the target of my affection. If first base is only ninety feet from home plate, how come each time I tried to score, I had to run a marathon? There just was not going to be any hanky-panky with this young lady. However, she was great fun.

Joe Cox, youngest of the Coxes, started dating Stephanie. One of our fun things to do was to go "pick a necking." We would pick up Dunkin' Donuts, spread a blanket in the park and neck. Thus, "pick a necking." Brookville Park, just over the Queens and Nassau County line, was a network of walking paths and green sloping lawns. A short stroll rendered the traffic sounds mute. As we powwowed around the baked goods, I took in Carol's attributes. She was well proportioned with a pure, smooth complexion, brown eyes, and light brown curly hair. All in all, I found her attractive, both in appearance and personality. Alternate nights were spent nursing a few beers and feeding the jukebox at Marlow's.

I showed up to work every day, cutting, bending, and grinding various shapes and sizes of steel. It was just short of assembly-line work and did not pay very much. I was unable to save any money while still hanging out with the gang. **Working and drinking, day after day, had been my dad's lifestyle and I was determined to do better.**

I am a 20-year-old living in my parents' apartment with my sister Claudia, a 14-year-old. Marilyn, Grace, Joan, and Paul had long since married and moved on. I had to find a way to do the same.

7. California, Here I Come

It was a quiet September night at Marlow's when Ed Curran, an old classmate from OLPH, came in with Rick Wynn. They had served together in the Marine Corps and were planning a trip to southern California, with a stop in Las Vegas, simply because they had never been there. I told them of the trip I had made to Fort Lewis and all the fun times we had. Over a few beers, a plan was hatched. I would join them and we would wait until my 21st birthday, on October 9, to leave. That way we would all be of legal age to gamble. We agreed to share the cost of gas and I would drive. I convinced Carol I had this need to go to California, and that if she were available when I returned, I would marry her. I don't know if I meant it, but I said it.

At the time, I was driving a 1953 Ford Crown Vic given to me by Tommy Remorse, Joan's husband. Just a "right place right time" kind of thing. The car was eight years old and the dealer wouldn't give him much as a trade, so he gave it to me. Of course, as luck would have it, on October 8th I blew the head gasket. I sold it to Richard Cox for 50 bucks.

The trip was still on, but the mode of transportation had changed to bus and thumb. We bought tickets to Springfield, Missouri. On the map that looked to be about halfway to Las Vegas.

What I did not know about my traveling companions was that they both thought that they were musicians when, in fact, they knew nothing about music. Ed had picked up a small saxophone and Rick had a guitar. They made noise all the way to Springfield, annoying every passenger on the bus.

Since continuing by bus was too expensive, we decided to hitchhike. Since we would be more likely to catch a ride individually, rather than as a threesome, we decided to split up. We walked to the highway and checked into a Motel 6 so that we could continue our trip, clean and fresh, the next morning. The plan was to wait in front of the Las Vegas YMCA at a predetermined time each day until all of us showed up.

The exit ramp from the truck stop was visible from our room. By a coin toss, we decided our batting order, Eddie first, Rick next, and then me. Rick watched from our room until Eddie had a ride. Then I waited until I saw Rick slip into a shiny new car. I then moved to the end of the rest area and waited and waited. After what seemed to be hours, a monster of a truck downshifted and pulled to the right. The hairy face under the ball cap growled, "Where you headed boy?"

"Las Vegas, sir."

"Oklahoma City, okay?"

"It's on the way."

"That it is, that it is. Climb in and put the bag behind you."

I had learned to drive a 2 1/2-ton truck in Germany, but this was much heavier. I watched as he shifted gears and then pulled a lever on the gear shift handle and continued. When I asked what the lever was for, he explained, "A split axle, I got 16 forward gears."

I wasn't any smarter for that explanation, but I was on my way to California via Vegas and felt relieved to be rolling. As we approached Oklahoma City, my new friend, Dan the truck driving man suggested I get out at the truck stop.

"There will be reefers heading west from here."

"What's a reefer?" I thought it was a marijuana cigarette.

"Refrigerated trucks. They'll be loaded with beef from the slaughterhouse."

I thanked him for the education and the introduction to his family, by way of photographs on the dashboard.

"Now, don't dillydally boy. They'll be gone after dinner!"

And then he was gone, working his way through all 16 gears again.

I did not get much of a look at Oklahoma City, only the truck stop and the highway. I did, however, note an abundance of cowboy hats. As I scarfed down a jumbo burger, I locked glances with a truck driver; my potential next ride.

"Hi!"

"Hey, y'all"

"Truck driver?" I asked.

"Yea," smiling, "You?" Knowing that I wasn't.

"No, I'm looking for a ride to Vegas."

"No guns, no drugs?"

"No guns, no drugs," I assured him.

"Okay, I'll get you to Albuquerque. One pit-stop in Amarillo then straight through. So, if you got to go, go now." I took his advice and was ready to board.

We told each other stories through the night. At times, perhaps, trying to outdo each other. The entire trip was in the dark so there wasn't much to see until about 4 a.m. when, on the horizon, lights spread out wider and wider.

"That's Albuquerque," he said. About an hour later, exhausted, we pulled into the truck stop where I was able to rent a small cubicle with a shower and a cot for six hours. Refreshed and fed by late afternoon, I set out for Gallup, Needles, and Vegas. The last leg was mostly riding in cars or pickups. By noon on the third day, I was looking for directions to the YMCA where Eddie and Rick were waiting for me.

There were no vacancies at the Y, so we shared a double room in a downtown hotel. Taking advantage of the inexpensive buffets, we managed to eat well. It was at one of those eateries that we met Mary and Sue, two daughters of a local wood worker whose business made fancy gambling tables for the casinos. They were amused with our New York stories and explained that Mary, the older of the two, was married to someone from New York, but it had not worked out and he returned to Long Island. The girls drove us out to the Strip to show us that part of Vegas that you cannot see from downtown. We hung out with them for the better part of two weeks, with no romantic complications, and spent most of our money.

Their father hooked us up with a lumber delivery truck that was making an overnight run to Santa Ana. It was a tight fit in the cab, but it was free, and we kept the driver awake. It was just past 2 a.m. when we pulled into the Columbia Lumberyard. We went into the office with the driver while he put his paperwork in the safe, then transferred to his car. He dropped us outside the 302 Cafe on Main Street, Santa Ana.

We pooled all our money and took a bus through Costa Mesa to Newport Beach. We found a cheap cottage to rent and somehow convinced the landlord we would not be any trouble. Despite a sincere effort to find work, after three weeks we were still unemployed, hungry, and dead broke. I talked my friends into making a food raid. I sent the former Marines out to steal a few potatoes and tomatoes from the outdoor market. They were only fifty percent successful, no tomatoes. I swiped a squeeze bottle of ketchup from a hot dog wagon and conjured up a field expedient meal of mashed potatoes and "tomatoes." This is pretty much how we survived until I found a day job parking cars across the street from city hall and the 302 Cafe.

We somehow managed the two weeks between paydays and with my tips we were able to eat a little better and I could afford to ride the bus to work. But by this time, Eddie was bummed out at having to hock his beloved saxophone and Rick was talking about going back to New York.

The commute from Newport Beach every day proved too much, so with my next paycheck, I parted company with my friends and moved into the Santa Ana Y. The Y seemed to be a magnet for gay men. I met an older resident, Peter, who had a car and offered to take me anyplace I needed to go. It was obvious he had ulterior motives, although he claimed not to. We remained friends and shared a ride to the laundromat each week.

The indoor pool was a bonus and very pleasant after parking cars all day, The only problem was that it supplied the gay men an opportunity to stroll around naked in the locker room. It reminded me of my days as a youth at the St. George Hotel in Brooklyn. That had been a mecca for gay men and pedophiles. More than once, I had been bumped, touched, or stared at while taking a shower. Despite the atmosphere, I had returned often. It was a one-fare zone on the A train, and for a few bucks, you could use the pool all day.

***

The Santa Ana Movie Theater was next to the 302 Cafe and each night a few movie-goers would take advantage of the open and unattended lot. My boss knew it but said it was not worth keeping the lot open at night for a few cars. A big thank you to the Hollywood movie industry. Exodus, Ben Hur, Psycho, and a few other blockbusters of 1959-60 were sold-out and the lot was nearly full each night. So, never one to pass up an opportunity to make a few bucks, I went into business for myself.

"Park it, lock it, enjoy the movie." I greeted my customers, collecting their five dollars each as they exited their cars. When the lot was full, I went home. Before long, the good movies made their exodus, and my night business was over.

Things went back to the same boring daytime routine until two detectives came on the lot. "Lawrence Phillips?" Other than my overtime swindle, I hadn't done anything wrong, so I owned up to being me.

"Yes, sir. What can I do for you?"

"You know Ed Curran?"

"Yes, but I haven't seen him in a few weeks. I took a room at the Y when I got this job and left them on the beach in Newport." After a series of questions involving a break-in at the Columbia Lumberyard, they were convinced that I had nothing to do with it. Neither they nor I knew the whereabouts of my two hungry friends and that was the last I ever heard of them.

Parking cars was getting old and I wanted a social life beyond the Y. I had met Lizzie, a single expectant mother, and several of her friends. She was nice but had enough trouble without me. I was going no place fast and found myself often thinking about New York. I decided to go back. After all, I had hitchhiked half-way across the states, why not all the way?

I called Mary and Sue in Vegas, told them I would be hitch hiking through on my way to New York, and hoped to see them. They were thrilled! As it happened, they too were planning a trip to Long Island to visit the former husband. They had the use of their dad's new Chrysler wagon and would welcome a man on board. I explained I was running on empty and could not help with the expenses.

"Not a problem. We have Daddy's credit card. Get to Vegas and you have a ride to your door."

Twenty-four hours later, we were headed east. At Kingman, Arizona we picked up Route 40 to Route10, taking the southern route to avoid any possible snow. On a cold, slushy country road in Opelousas, Louisiana, with both girls asleep in the back of the wagon, I slid across the center line and hit an oncoming car. When we stopped spinning and sliding, I was on the shoulder with the nose of the wagon nearly in the swamp. Using all my strength, pressing the brake pedal to the floor, I barked for the girls to get out before we slipped in. I was surprised when I gradually re-leased the brake and the car did not move. It was a long time standing in the freezing rain, the three of us and the other driver before we could see the red lights flashing in the distance. The sheriff's deputy told the three of us to get in his car while he called for a wrecker; leaving the other driver, an elderly black man, standing in the cold night rain. Holding the radio microphone to his mouth, "I need a wrecker down here. Dis nigger run those young folks off the road."

"No, no," I said, "I hit him. I crossed over the line."

"Boy, you sit there and shut your mouth." The officer's tone brokering no argument.

After routine paperwork, we were on our way with only cos-metic damage to the car. We could not help but wonder what would happen to the poor black man. A summons, jail time, stand-ing in the rain all night? There was nothing we could do to help.

***

Two days later I was delivered to Ozone Park and the girls went hunting for the husband on Long Island.

At home, the word on the street was that Josephine was pregnant. What's more, supposedly, I was the responsible party.

This is bull! The baby cannot be mine and Josephine knows it. She was a neighborhood girl who had put herself in my path several times before I left for the west coast. I admit that I had accepted an invitation from her to visit while her father was at work, but that went nowhere. We had gone straight to her bedroom and were a half-second from doing the deed when her father returned. I had slipped into my pants and followed as Josephine directed me into the bathroom. She ran the water and called down to her father that she was about to get in the shower. I hid behind the shower curtain with my shoes in one hand and my other fist cocked and ready to defend myself if need be. Thank goodness, her father left the house. That had been my only encounter with Josephine.

According to the guys in the neighborhood, she had been with several of them. Some had been approached by her father, who was more than just upset. He vowed to find the boy responsible for Josephine's pregnancy. This was not the reception committee I expected after driving 3000 miles.

I knew the best way to confront the situation was to confront her father directly. I called him first. "Hello Mr. Napoli, this is Larry Phillips."

"Oh, you're the one who ran off to California!"

"I did not run off. The trip was planned well in advance. I just returned a few days ago and I assure you I have not as much as kissed Josephine."

He threatened me several times, while I tried to defuse the situation. At one point I offered to sit down with him to prove my innocence. How I was going to do that was a puzzle, but I offered.

"Mr. Napoli, I'll come over now, if you promise you'll keep your hands in your pockets. I'll take you on your word, sir. Do we have a deal?"

He replied in the affirmative.

I rang the doorbell and waited thinking, *Phillips you have more balls than brains*. Nervously, I stood two steps down on the red brick stoop. The door swung open to reveal, centered in the door frame, the biggest lumberjack of a man I had ever seen. As I ascended and entered the living room, his physique seemed to diminish. He stood erect looking at me, with both hands firmly in his pockets. Okay, had he taken my request literally, or was he concealing a handgun?

"I'm sorry for your trouble." I started.

"You should be sorry."

"No, I'm not apologizing. I feel bad that this is happening to Josephine and your family. I talked to the guys and I can assure you..." *Be careful Phillips. You are in dangerous territory. No, do not go there, idiot!*

"You can assure me of what?" he demanded.

My heart beat faster, harder, and louder. I could feel it in my ears and throat, and my mouth was dry.

"Some of the guys told me they had been with your daughter and would be willing to testify to the fact..."

I knew the moment the words left my mouth that I was in deep shit.

"You better get the F@#K out of my house!"

I did not think twice. I exited, hoping he did not have a pistol in his pocket.

***

About three days later, I heard from Sue and Mary. They had located the former husband and were headed back to Vegas. Was I interested? It did not take me long to decide. I needed a day to say goodbye to the Lee sisters, especially Carol. For some reason, I felt the need to reaffirm my offer of marriage, if I ever came back.

I also needed to get some cash. I hit my father up, and he gave me the only $20 bill he had. I told my traveling partners I was still tapped out. No problem, Daddy's credit card was still working.

Lastly, I decided to call Lizzie who was now the proud mother of a baby girl. I told her I would be back in town looking for work and asked if I could stay with her. It was a one-bedroom apartment, more correctly, a converted motel room in Santa Ana.

She said "Yeah I could use some company. The baby may keep you up."

"Beats the streets. Thank you."

***

Driving most of the way gave me a lot of time to figure out what I was going to do for income...duh? Zipping south on the Jersey Turnpike, the industrial buildings clipped by like dominoes put in place to guide commerce and industry in the north and southerly direction.

What the hell was I doing? I had not even looked for a job. I had been in town less than a week and I was off and running again. It was the third trip across the country in less than six months and I was doing it on someone else's dime. I would be lucky if I didn't get arrested for vagrancy in some small town out west.

I had a small canvas bag with a few changes of underwear, but no place to shower and change. What was I doing? Escaping Josephine's father or running away from Carol? I was looking for something, but I did not know what. Suddenly, I realized I was daydreaming. I had better keep my eyes on the road. This car and Daddy's credit card were the only things keeping me from becoming a highway vagrant.

We returned to Vegas using a co-pilot, in the front seat, and the third person sleeping in the back of the wagon. We rotated every few hours and thus kept the driver awake and alert.

Tuesday afternoon, after freshening up at the girls' apartment, I grabbed a ride with a trucker. Arriving Wednesday morning I thanked the trucker and walked the half-mile to Lizzie's place. After a short reunion, she noticed my fatigue and offered me the bed for a few hours of rest.

I awoke to feel her soft hands stroking my face. "Hungry?"

"What's on the menu?"

"I have some leftovers."

"You shouldn't refer to yourself as leftovers." She smiled.

"It's spaghetti from Dino's down the block."

A glimmer of laughter came into her eyes. "Maybe dessert."

We shared the pasta from the aluminum pan while catching up. It was as close to a family day as I had in a long time. I rather enjoyed it and told her so. The baby was washed, changed, and settled in the porta-crib. Liz and I sat on the worn-out love seat, put our feet on the coffee table, finding comfort and found security in each other's embrace.

After a week with no promise of gainful employment, I started to see myself as a gigolo. Walking down Main Street, I passed the recruiting station. A large poster in the window depicted mean-looking, serious warriors on an inflatable boat, carrying weapons I did not recognize. They were recruiting Special Forces volunteers who would undergo extensive training to include being "jump" qualified. In my former Army life, I always said that if I reenlisted, I would want to be a soldier's soldier. One of the best. Determined to be the best I could be."

That night, though comfortable and secure with Liz, I was nagged by indecisiveness. Then the epiphany! I could go back on active duty and make it a career. I have three years in already. I could do three more and evaluate it then. If it went well, I'd have six years toward retirement. By daylight, I had made up my mind to at least inquire.

Recruiters are always starched, shined, and alert. They rose to their feet the moment I opened the door "Good morning, sir."

"Good morning Sargent, Specialist." Addressing them by rank gave them an inkling of my prior service.

"What can we do for you?"

"I'm thinking of re-upping."

"How long are you out?" they asked.

"About a year and three months." That started the ball rolling. I expressed my desire for an assignment with Special Forces.

"Well, they are expanding, and we have slots open if you qualify."

"What have I got to do to be guaranteed a spot?"

"First, pass a test. Mostly multiple guesses, take the test first, if you fail, you can pick some other field you're qualified for, or not re-up."

"What about rank?"

"You've been out too long to retain your specialist fourth rating you'll be an E-2 but you should move up quickly because of your prior service."

"Let me take the SF qualifier first. Then I'll decide."

I took the test that afternoon, which included visual perception and spatial ability. The questions were based on photos taken at different angles and observations from the photos; things I considered to be common sense. It had several parts and took about two hours plus time to be corrected.

I walked down to the 302 Cafe for coffee where I met two gay hairdressers I had known from my days parking cars across the street. I told them of my plans and they tried to talk me out of them. They invited me to join them for dinner that evening but I said I would have to pass. It was obvious there was more than one recruiter on the block. I returned to the recruiter's office to hear the good news. I could be guaranteed the schools if I passed all the training to include jump school. I was sworn in the next day and on the train to Fort Ord, south of Salinas.

The train accommodated many men, women, and children and about a hundred boys, soon to become men. The range of emotions in the recruits ran from their last ride in freedom to a great adventure. Others sat silently in obvious contemplation. There was much chatter among those who had been told war stories by their elders or family members. Each of them knew more than the next guy. I knew they would all find the truth and fit snugly within it by the end of the next eight weeks.

The buses were standing by to take us to the reception center where the training officers were standing by to guide the new arrivals. The screaming and ridicule started at once.

"You're in the Army now. Move it!"

"Lineup, look alive."

"Does your mother know you're out this late?"

The chaos went on until all the troops were assigned a bunk and footlocker. The mattresses were folded in thirds, with blankets, sheets, and a pillow on top of each footlocker. A young buck sergeant called for attention. His first job was to instruct the proper position of attention and how each of us was to stand at the edge of the footlocker. It was kind of amusing watching the kids, some of whom did not know their left from their right. This sergeant was having a ball, pointing out their lack of military bearing. The confusion slowly started to fade as we all got acclimated to military life.

Induction was a three-day process consisting of haircuts, physicals, shots, uniform issue, and instruction on how to wear it. Then next came orientation and assignment to training groups. Day four was the first day of basic training. This is when you get to know each other; the weak, the strong, the homesick, the smart-mouthed, and the know-it-all. Then, there were the few who had never been naked in front of another person, neither male nor female. Day by day they all changed; their inhibitions faded away as boys became men. Some doing things they had never thought they were capable of. Having been down this road before made it interesting.

Basic training was optional for me, but I decided to retake it for a few reasons. First, it had been five years since I took my first basic, freezing my ass off at Fort Dix. Second, I was a long way from my peak physical condition. Third, I was destined for paratrooper school and then on to what was to be a career in Army Special Forces where physical and mental acuity were a must. Failure at any phase of training would put my dreams and career in a tailspin.

Bill Halberstadt was an excellent recruit. It was apparent that he came from a good family. He displayed respect and a willingness to learn. Once he found out I had prior service, he began asking me about various things. I did not mind helping him because he wasn't a smart ass and generally wanted to do what was right. Sometimes he would talk about Maggie, the hometown girl he left behind. It was strange to hear a guy referring to a girl with such outspoken respect and reverence. Never an utterance of locker room language. No "F this" and "F that." Except for one night after a live-fire exercise, Bill crawled out from under the barbed wire all wet and covered with mud, and said, "Holy shit that was f@#k!!g wild."

"Oh yes, it sure as shit was and, by the way, the profanity police are off duty."

At the end of basic training, it is customary to receive two weeks' leave. Bill, knowing I was from New York, invited me to stay with him at his parents' home in San Francisco. I initially turned him down, even though I knew that staying behind would probably see me spending my two weeks doing menial details around the training group.

One evening after training, Bill and I walked to the PX hoping that a cold beer would relieve the aches and pains of the day's activities. He went to the pay phone, while I sipped a 3.2 beer. I couldn't help but think that it was like water compared to the German brew.

"Larry," Bill gestured from the phone booth. "My mother wants to speak to you."

"Hello, Mrs. Halberstadt. How are you?"

"I'm fine, thank you. Bill tells me you don't want to come home with him."

Her voice was flowered with good breeding and measured with perfect enunciation. I started babbling, making up excuses on the fly about how I didn't want to be in the way.

"Nonsense. You'll have your own room and bath."

To stall for time to come up with a good reason not to go, I ended with, "Sounds swell. Can I think about it?"

She made a tsking noise "Nothing to think about. I'll see you at the graduation ceremony. Bye now."

And with that, it was settled. I was to spend two weeks at the Halberstadts'.

Commencement day came and the troops were marched out onto the parade ground and presented to their friends and family. The final command, "Troops dismissed."

Everyone broke from formation to the applause of the crowd. Mrs. Halberstadt was tall, smartly dressed, middle-aged, and pleasant. She also had a sense of humor which made me believe we were going to have a good two weeks together.

"Mr. Halberstadt had to remain in San Francisco at his studio; working to meet a deadline. You will meet him at dinner later this evening."

It was a pleasant ride in their late-model Cadillac, driving north through San Francisco and across the Golden Gate Bridge. We laughed and joked along the way about the difference in the ride between this Sedan de Ville and the two-and-a-half-ton truck that the Army used to transport us. Approaching Marin County, I remembered hearing somewhere that it was one of the wealthiest counties in the country. We traversed the winding hills, seeing the homes with their exquisite landscaping. We pulled into a crushed stone circular driveway in front of a two-story colonial. The house was nestled in the side of a steep incline. "Well, we're home," she said as we exited the car.

The home and the community were undeniably beautiful. The front of the house faced rolling hills that were lush with foliage. It resembled no place I had ever seen before, and a long cry from our three-room apartment in Queens. I knew right then that if we did absolutely nothing, I would have a great time just being there.

Entering through the leaded glass double doors into a marble foyer, there was a table in the center, adorned with a large vase full of fresh flowers. To the left was a beautiful mahogany staircase. We moved through the foyer to a family room attached to what appeared to be a catering kitchen. There were yards of counter tops, a large center island, and tall kitchen cabinets. The spotless stainless-steel appliances and sparkling chrome water taps were state of the art and shone like silver jewelry. This kitchen was set up for some serious cooking. Even the spice jars were arranged alphabetically. I said to myself, *this ain't no mess hall*.

After some refreshing soft drinks, Bill took me down to our new quarters; Bill's room and a guest room, joined by a shared bath. The guest room furnishings were highly polished, the quilted bed covers matched the draperies, and an easy chair sat in the corner. The plush carpeting seemed to cry out *take off your shoes and feel my pile between your toes*. Bill's room was that of a typical teenager with its clutter of baseball stuff, golf clubs, and music albums. His furniture had seen some wear and tear, but it was still comfortable.

An hour or so had passed when Bill's father arrived. I greeted him, "Mr. Halberstadt, it's a pleasure to meet you. Thank you very much for inviting me to spend some time in your beautiful home."

"Glad to have you here. I hope you enjoy your vacation and, by the way, call me Mr. H."

Awkwardly, "Okay, Mr. H."

During a pleasant cocktail hour, we shared "war stories" of the previous eight weeks. Mrs. H. worked feverishly about the kitchen, as Mr. H. explained that he was an illustrations photographer and had a studio downtown. He planned to take us there the next day and I was excited. I had never seen San Francisco. Although I tried not to stare, Mr. H. caught me glancing where three fingers of his left hand were missing. He explained that he had lost them in World War II when his plane was shot down. I thanked him for his sacrifice and the conversation returned to other subjects until it was time for dinner.

Noticing the table was set for eight, I asked if they were expecting company. "Oh yes, our neighbors, the Boddins, are coming. They should be here in a few minutes."

And then the Boddins arrived with their daughter, Cappi, and the term "OMG" came into being. "Oh, my God!" I swallowed hard, OMG again. She could have stepped out of a fashion magazine. White heels met the ankle-length white pants, clicking out visions of freshly starched sheets. The blue button-down blouse had short puffy sleeves and a turned-up collar, all pulled together by a red patent leather belt. I could only assume that the patriotic ensemble had been deliberately put together for Bill and me. The latest addition to the nation's arsenal. I was mindful that I was a guest and could not screw up or make a fool of myself, which I had been known to do.

Before any introductions were made, the loud rumble of a muffler could be heard out on the stone driveway. "Maggie's here!" Bill leaped from his seat and double-timed to open the front door, as I sized up the Boddins. He was a Sasquatch-looking man with a full beard. If not for the white-on-white tailor-made shirt, I would have thought him to be a Harley leather-vest kind of guy. His wife was barely 5 feet tall, about 125 to 130 pounds, and casually dressed.

Returning after what must have been a long welcoming kiss, Bill and Maggie entered the dining room with telltale smiles on their faces.

Then the formal introductions, "Larry, meet Dr. and Mrs. John Boddin."

"Call me Joan," she piped in.

Extending my hand across the table, "Pleasure to meet you both."

"This is our daughter, Cappi."

I reached out to the gorgeous imitation of an American flag. Her hands were soft, and her nails manicured with white tips.

Forcing my attention away, "You must be Maggie," I said to the latest arrival. "I've heard a lot about you in the last eight weeks. All good, I might add."

Turning to Bill, "Every bit as pretty as you said."

Maggie was pleasant, but not the looker that Cappi was. Her faded jeans and yellow turtleneck seemed to say, "Look I've grown while you were gone." And look he did. Several times during dinner, I caught him glancing at her nicely shaped breasts as we sat opposite the girls, with the parents to our right.

The air became filled with the aroma of the standing rib roast, Yorkshire pudding, string beans almondine, and zinfandel gravy. Occasionally a whiff of Cappi's fragrance would make its way across the table and linger beneath my nostrils as an intermezzo. Dinner progressed without incident. The napkin on my lap, the proper fork at the proper time. I was trying so hard to make the best impression.

When Cappi offered to clear the table, I jumped up to help. While washing dishes, I realized that she was not only beautiful but also pleasant and intelligent. Her every move was graceful. I thought I would gladly eat a plate of dog food just to wash dishes with her again.

Later that evening, I mentioned to Bill my observations of Cappi.

"Did you make a date with her?" Bill asked.

"No."

"Stupid! You should have. That's why she came to dinner. Call and invite her to come with us to Chinatown on Monday."

I made the call with great trepidation, steeling myself for rejection. But as I stumbled out the invite, she accepted with enthusiasm. My heart was off to the races. I quickly spun around, tangling the phone cord around my upper torso, as I fist-pumped the air with excitement. "Okay, then I'll see you Monday."

***

I had not known what to expect on our visit to the studio, but the space far exceeded my expectations. It was in a large warehouse with high ceilings and skylights which allowed the natural light to fill the space. It appeared to contain all the props for every TV commercial I had ever seen. There was one perfect replica of a number two pencil, only it was 35 feet long and hung ten feet above our heads. In another area, a photo shoot was in progress, which just happened to be a beer commercial. There were cases of beer on ice with dozens of glasses chilled at different temperatures to achieve the ultimate cascading foam and frost at just the right angle and in the perfect light. If the photo was not optimal, then the beer was discarded. We drank a lot of beer that day and, while watching, I thought of my father who would never, never, ever pour beer down the drain.

Chinatown was great! We walked the streets, shopped little stores, and toured the fortune cookie factory. Everyone laughed when I pretended that mine said "You have already found your fortune." A section with colorfully painted balconies and fire escapes was especially interesting. New York's Chinatown was not so artistically enhanced. I ducked into a store and bought Cappi a Chinese fan. I gave it to her, exclaiming that she needed it because she was so hot looking. That garnered a flirtatious smile. It was truly a day to remember. Her black pedal pushers and white sweater only served to accent her well-proportioned figure. The oversized sunglasses hid what I already knew to be beautiful blue eyes. Her champagne blond hair glistened in the California sun. I took her arm as we approached some rough-looking kids on the crowded sidewalk. After they passed, I let my hand slide down to hers. She squeezed mine and pulled closer. Our hands stayed there the rest of the day.

The days that followed were magnificent. The four of us visited Fisherman's Wharf, the sea lions, and rode the cable car to Telegraph Hill. We traversed Lombard Street, the most crooked street in the country. The days in the city, evenings with friends, dinner with family, all this truly was the most wonderful vacation.

When back at the Boddin house, we were encouraged to hang out in the family room. It was in a separate part of the house with a beige shag rug, comfortable leather chairs, oak tables, and a console television. Highlighting the room was a large, padded window seat in a bay window overlooking the hills and pastures that sloped down toward San Francisco. The overstuffed sofa faced the window, set that way to admire the view. Behind the loveseat was a three-foot table supporting a portable stereo record player and a large collection of 33 RPMs on the shelf below. We selected the music for the evening, then moved the arm so that the latest Johnny Mathis record would play over and over.

One night, Cappi and I dozed off in each other's arms. The next day, when Mrs. Boddin told Cappi they had stopped by to say good night, but we were already sleeping, we assumed their conspicuous absences meant they considered us to be trustworthy adults. It was during those late nights that we got to know each other. We would sit and talk until the sun came up. Then we would kiss to seal the end of another beautiful day and I would quietly exit the house. Crossing the street, I would enter the Halberstadts' through the private entrance to the rooms downstairs. This became a nightly routine and no one seemed to mind at all.

One night I stirred up enough courage to tell her how perfect I thought she was. She laughed lightly and said, "Thank you, but I disagree."

I quickly rose from the sofa, went down on my knees, and looked straight into her electric blue eyes. "Pay attention to me." With the setting sun illuminating her milky white skin, I started, "Your perfect diamond-shaped face is framed by your sparkling blond hair." She smiled as I used two fingers to point out her forehead. "Your eyebrows are full in the center and taper to the ends." I continued in my journey "Your eyes are like a laser, pale blue with a ring of indigo, surrounded by porcelain with butterfly lashes that flutter out messages of desire." She started to speak. I gently placed my fingers over her lips and went on. "Cupid left his bow resting on your puffy upper lip, which turns up at the ends, causing you to have a perpetual smile."

"You have studied me," she said.

"Yes, I have, from your cheekbone to your pointy little chin, and I must tell you, that you are as beautiful on the inside as you are on the outside. It's going to be hard to suit up and go back. I'm falling in love with you."

She reached out with both hands, leaned forward, and pulled me close until our lips met. I was certain that she felt the same way. Is there language in a kiss? If there is, this one was telling a long story. She had expressed her love for her parents, her plans for college followed by medical school, and her firm commitment to remaining a virgin until marriage. And for the first time in my life, I was truly okay with that.

When the kiss ended, she whispered my name. "I'm afraid you'll forget about me. That once you leave you won't even call or write." I vowed to return and promised I would come back on my free weekends, even if I had to hitchhike.

"Because you are unforgettable," and I started to do my best Nat King Cole impression.

On the eve of our departure, Bill to Fort Devens, Massachusetts, and me back to Fort Ord, the Halberstadts treated us to dinner. Bill, Maggie, Cappi, and I squeezed into the 1963 Caddy and joked about it being our "last supper," of sorts. Vacation is over, I thought, as we arrived in front of a brick building, outlined with peanut lights. I took a deep breath and felt my lungs expand with the salty moisture of Frisco Bay. Mr. H. led us through the black wrought iron gate and down two steps where a tall oak-paneled door opened, and we were greeted by a six-foot-tall, gray-haired maître d'. "Good evening, Mr. and Mrs. Halberstadt."

I took in my surroundings. The wait staff was adorned in tuxedos and the wine room, encased in glass, extended up to the second floor. Visible through the glass, one penguin type was putting on a tableside show with a flaming liqueur, which I later came to know as Bananas Foster.

It was obvious that the Halberstadts were regulars, as they were greeted by name by three different individuals. Bill and I were in uniform and the girls were dressed to kill. Maggie wore a black pants suit with a ruffled white blouse, four-inch heels, and dangling earrings. Cappi on the other hand, OMG again, brown heels, one of which she kicked off so she could play footsie with me under the table. The footwear supported and shaped her legs until they disappeared under the hem of her knee-length mocha skirt. Above was a light gold, diaphanous blouse, displaying a fair amount of her bosom and the valley that ran between them. At the apex snuggled a single teardrop diamond pendant with matching earrings. The last two weeks with this unsoiled, unpretentious, seductive angel had my testosterone factories working overtime.

Dinner ended all too soon. For two hours or so I was enjoying the good life. The ride home was a verbal recap of the past two weeks during which I continued to express my gratitude, perhaps too much, until Mr. H. said, "Larry, we get it and we're happy for you."

I did not want the night to end. We said our goodnights to Mr. and Mrs. H. and crossed the street to Cappi's so I could say goodbye to the Boddins. We sat with them for an hour and a half until a gentle nudge from Cappi caused me to note the time. I gradually ended the conversation with more expressions of appreciation. Together, we headed to the lower level. As I turned to make one last statement, she pulled my arm to move me along. She whispered, "It's late and we only have a few hours to be alone.

"But I wanted to tell them how blessed they are to have you and I would like to share in that blessing… and that I love you."

"Larry, they know all that."

"How?"

"I told them."

"And they're okay with that?"

She nodded. "Cappi, I have to tell you something. You have taken my heart; you are all I can think about. I want to be with you 24 hours a day, seven days a week. I'm constantly planning our future together."

I had said similar things to girls before. Now I meant it and I feared that fate would turn the tables on me and give me a taste of my own medicine.

"Hey, where were you? You just went blank and pale. Are you okay?"

"Yes, I'm fine I just thought that I... I don't want anything to happen to us."

"Like what?" she asked.

"You know, maybe you'll meet someone else or something, I don't know."

"Not going to happen."

"You sure?"

"Yep, yep, yep. Now kiss me you fool."

"Yep."

Settling into the sofa, her skirt slipped up to mid-thigh, I removed my uniform jacket and placed it over the back of the chair, opened my collar, and removed my tie. Her almost transparent blouse was now pulling at the buttons, the pendant glistened. It was not the jewelry that had my heart rate on the increase. The evening progressed, alternately with deep conversation and petting. Coming dangerously close to shattering her long-held commitment to virginity.

The sun rose to stain the hillside in shades of crimson and gold. We shared our last embrace. I whispered, "You are so beautiful and I'll keep that vision with me until I return."

8. Return to Fort Ord and Beyond

It was a damp, drizzly day when I exited the taxi at the Trail-ways bus depot.

Where is the California sun when I need it? Quickly, I passed through the exhaust fumes hoping not to pick up the smell of diesel on my new uniform. Looking up the two steps at the over-weight, middle-aged bus driver, "San Francisco?" I was headed back to Marin County. My commanding officer had granted me a 48-hour compassionate pass. "Climb on."

I placed my overnight bag on the shelf above my seat and slumped against the window, two rows behind the driver. The bus accelerated with a low growl which gradually rose to a high whine. The large, tinted windows presented a panoramic view of the countryside. We cruised north through Salinas, the salad cap-ital of the world, and then San Jose.

As the bus zipped through the countryside, I became mesmer-ized by the clicking of the rubber expansion joints, the tapping rhythm of the road, and the broken white lines. After a while, I turned my gaze from the window to the newspaper in my lap. I started to tear up, clinching the paper in an effort at self-control. I turned back to the road and the vague awareness of my reflection in the tinted window. I pushed back a tear concerned that it wouldn't look good in uniform. Yeah, grown men do not cry. A million thoughts rushed through my mind, but I could not hold on to a single one.

Once again, I forced my attention back to the newspaper article and the details of the accident. "Vehicle loses control, hits tree." The extent of the injuries was not clear. I recognized the mangled, late-model Mercedes sports car in the photograph, having seen it in the Boddin garage.

When I had commented on it, Cappi had said, "Oh, that's my father's baby, no one gets to drive his baby but him."

My mind was in turmoil, my thoughts scattered. That beautiful machine mangled in a tree. Why was he speeding, had he been drinking, was someone else at fault? Too many questions and along with them my imaginings of the sequence of events, like a film on fast forward. I forced myself to focus on better times and returned to the cadence of the highway.

I had vowed to return to Cappi. Never did I think for one moment, it would be after only two days. I had left San Francisco with orders to return to the Fort Ord training regimen for advanced heavy weapons training. I had no address or phone number, and so no way for anyone to reach me. It was just happenstance that I had even learned of the accident. On my way to the latrine, I grabbed a paper and saw the small article on page five below the fold. "A family returning from the beach lost control, hitting a tree. It was uncertain what caused the accident, but a CHiPs spokesman said speed was a factor. Estimated to be doing 55 miles per hour, which is 15 miles above the local limit. Items recovered at the scene indicated the family was returning from the beach. All three occupants were taken to Holy Mother Hospital. Later identified as Dr. and Mrs. Boddin and their daughter. All residing on Hilltop Lane, San Rafael, Marin County." The family outing had been in the planning stages the day before I left. We had talked about it and how both of us wished I could also be there.

I had a short layover in San Francisco, to change buses, where I grabbed a cup of coffee and a fresh newspaper. Searching for an update on the accident, I found it on the page with the obituaries. I could feel the blood drain from my face and I grew lightheaded. The waitress, a matronly lady, approached, drying her hands on her apron, and asked, softly "Hey, soldier, are you all right?"

I said I was, but I was not. The one person who had given me purpose, and changed my jangled life, was gone. I felt as if I had swallowed a tennis ball. Air could not get into my lungs and exhaling gave me a riveting pain in my chest. I had never experienced anything quite like this. My mental state had affected my physical being. I had to pull myself together. I stepped into the john, grasping the edge of the sink, I looked in the mirror. You look like hell! I splashed my face with cold water and dried it with a paper towel. Running my fingers through the short stubble that was my hair, I focused on controlling my breathing and exited the restroom. I found a clean area on the long wooden bench and waited for my bus to San Rafael. I reminisced of times with Cappi; a romantic afternoon in a Japanese Garden, riding on the cable car hanging out the sides like two kids on a merry-go-round.

I guessed the city bus to be a 1950 vintage; reminding me of the Green Line buses I rode in Queens. The driver jockeyed for position on the city streets and headed for the Golden Gate Bridge. I was drawn back to my first crossing, just two weeks prior. The bus stopped and the driver announced San Rafael. The clicking of the handbrake was my signal, like a bell to a prize fighter. I was on my way into a ring of emotional pugilism without any experience or training.

Determined to be as strong as I could, I took one more look at the newspaper. Skimming through the story, I found the address of the funeral home and asked for directions from a local storekeeper. As I plodded along, each step brought increased anxiety. I could feel my pulse throbbing in my neck. What could I say? What would I say? I entered O'Rourke's Funeral Home and was greeted by two attendants.

"Boddin family?" I inquired.

"Yes, sir. Down the hall, the last chapel on the right."

It was a long hall with a tall ceiling and stained-glass skylights, much like a church. Every few feet were marble tables with lamps that cast wide circles of light on the plush carpeting. The silence was broken by an occasional voice or sniffling from the other chapels. I arrived at the door labeled "Boddin," set my bag down outside the door, took a deep breath, and entered.

Mr. and Mrs. H. stood up, surprised to see me.

"How on earth? We had no way of contacting you."

Mrs. Boddin was hardly recognizable. She was in a wheel-chair, one arm and one leg in a cast, and massive bandages swathing her head. The Halberstadts continued to speak, but I could only extend my hand, palm out, gesturing them to stop. I could not utter a word.

I stepped up to the closed, beautifully crafted wooden casket. The scent of flowers seemed to drift up around me, but there were none. I recognized the fragrance as the same one I had detected the first night I met her. It brought with it a sudden sense of calm. I had become relaxed, as I had always been when I was in her presence. Had this come from her? Is that even possible? I had called her an angel many times, and perhaps now she was one. All I knew was that I would have given anything just to hold her one more time and to see her beautiful smile.

Dear God, I started. Oh, this is silly. I mean, I know God. After all, I went to Catholic school, but some things even God... I stopped myself. I stood there for a minute or two and I put my hand on the lid of the coffin. What should have been firm and smooth under my hand felt soft and fluffy like a quilted bed cover. My hand continued to enter deeper into the softness. I felt at peace like never before. Light and transparent, my hand came to rest on Cappi's cheek. She was warm and supple. Heavenly music came from inside the casket. I turned to ask if anyone else had heard it, but the room was empty. She and I were alone again. I traced two fingers across her forehead, down the bridge of her nose, and lightly over her lips to that pretty little chin. God had allowed me to touch an angel! The slow withdrawal of my hand signaled a silent mournful goodbye.

I turned again to find Mrs. Boddin and the Halberstadts back in the room. A short conversation revealed that Dr. Boddin had had too much to drink, causing the accident, and had succumbed to his injuries earlier that morning. While I felt sorry for the loss of a husband, a neighbor, a friend; I was full of rage for his killing Cappi.

I sat for several hours, reminiscing, and beating up on God. Why did he take her so young? She was so good, spiritual, honest, and respectful. Certainly, she was heaven bound and wasn't that a far better place. I started to realize that God knows what he is doing, and who am I to second-guess the Almighty? I dried my eyes and thanked everyone for their hospitality and the part they had played in bringing Cappi and me together and allowing our relationship to develop.

Wishing everyone well, I left the chapel, picking up my bag and the newspaper. I scanned it again, reading once more of speed and booze which sent two adults to the hospital; the daughter de-capitated and pronounced dead at the scene. At last, I could read it without tearing up or the feeling of a tennis ball in my chest.

The California sun was setting as I briskly walked back to the bus stop, passing a music store. The lyrics of "Unforgettable" wafted from inside the store… "unforgettable that's what you are." I dropped the paper in the trashcan. Like the words of the song, recollections of my brief time with Cappi filled my head.

***

The next eight weeks were jam-packed with information on mortars, recoilless rifles, rocket launchers (bazookas), and gre-nade launchers. I made several phone calls to the Halberstadts, but the most difficult was to Joan Boddin, whose whole world had been suddenly and irreversibly torn apart. I was grateful for the privacy of a phone booth because we were both crying and be-moaning our love for Cappi.

I made one last visit to San Rafael, the day I completed the advanced course. Joan and I had a long leisurely lunch together, reminiscing. She acknowledged that she knew I had respected Cappi's wishes to remain untouched and expressed her apprecia-tion for holding her daughter in such high regard. With watery eyes and an emotional hug, that lasted long enough to attract at-tention, I once again felt her presence through her mother's em-brace.

***

I always looked up to my brother. Paul was my idol in every-thing. At play in the street and when it came to weightlifting, he was my idol. He was also my "go-to guy" on how to talk to girls. But never was I more impressed than when he came home in his paratrooper uniform. He shined from head to toe, his khakis starched and pressed with razor-sharp creases; pants bloused over his spit-shined boots. Even the leather laces were shined. Jump school had not been a possibility during my first tour. I was simply glad to get off the court docket and onto the Army payroll.

But this time it was different. I was determined to get my wings and make my brother proud of me. While jump school was only three weeks long, it proved to be my greatest physical challenge. Knowing how fatiguing it would be, I had done extra PT in the prior 16 weeks of training. And when the time came, I was ready, both physically and mentally.

Fort Benning is in the southwest corner of Georgia, an area nobody just happens to pass through. You must want to get there. You head down Interstate 85 toward Montgomery, Alabama. At La Grange, you take a hard turn to the south onto I 185. A few miles later, after you pass through Columbus, you hit Route 27. The front gate is literally at the end of the road, but it represents the beginning of the journey for those who want to become air-borne troopers.

I was greeted by Sargent Rucker. "Soldier, what are you?"

"Airborne! Sargent."

"No, you are not."

"AIRBORNE!" was the response to everything, and if not, it was "All the Way" or "Airborne all the way."

"Look at you with your hands on your hips. Don't you know only prostitutes and fags put their hands on their hips? Which one are you? Give me ten."

Ten push-ups were the standard punishment for the slightest infraction or sometimes for nothing at all. Sargent Rucker was black, dark black, 6 feet tall, double-wide between the shoulders, and narrow at the waist.

I was issued a helmet (steel pot) with three numbers on it, "413".

"You! Blue eyes what's your name?"

"Phillips, Sargent."

"No from now on you are "413." You do not deserve a name. If you ever get your wings, you can have your name back. Till then you are just "413." Are you sure you're not a fag?"

"Yes, Sargent."

***

Fort Benning, originally Camp Benning before World War I, had the mission of training infantry troops. By WW II it was the home of the Airborne. In the middle of the post is a large parade area with several odd-looking pieces of training equipment. These include three 250-foot-tall towers that had come from a fairground in Brooklyn. Along with the towers were mockups of various airplanes. At one end of the parade ground was the headquarters of the First Battalion of the 507th Airborne Infantry Regiment which runs the US Army Airborne School, more affectionately known as Jump School.

The schooling consisted of 125 classroom hours plus physical training. Week one is ground week, followed by week two, tower training. Then, those who have survived the punishing runs, temperature, humidity, and screaming cadre of trainers, will exit a plane … in flight.

Each day started at 6 a.m. with an exhausting run. You would think that was a good idea, but at Fort Benning, it is anything but. Most of the year, but especially in the summer months, the sunrise temperatures are above 80 and the humidity is the same. The run is followed by the "daily dozen." Twelve repetitions of twelve exercises to strengthen the entire body. By this time, sheets of muscle had formed around the trellis of my bones.

During week one, the students became familiar with their new equipment and with basic exit/landing procedures. Other than the metaphysical, it focuses on the various parachute landing falls (PLFs). Those are essentially tumbling exercises designed to allow a trooper to safely land in a variety of different conditions and terrains. For example, the proper PLF for landing on soft dirt or grass is to land with knees bent and to roll in the direction the parachute is pulling. Attempting to land stiff and rigid will only result in broken bones.

Along with the PLF training, we spent a lot of time on the 34-foot tower. The three-story towers are much like the ones used by the US Park Service to watch out for forest fires. They are used to familiarize troops with the forces and feelings they will experience when they start jumping out of actual planes.

The instructor starts by fitting you with a six-point harness and a set of risers. The harness is a tight fit, especially around the groin area. This is essential to avoid a debilitating personal injury to the male students. If you get my meaning! After you are all fitted you walk up several flights of stairs to the top of the tower. The instructor attaches the risers to a wire which runs from an exit door to the base of the large steel pole approximately 100 yards away. Now, you just step off from the edge of the platform while focusing on a landmark in the distance.

A bit apprehensive, I approached the exit door and stepped off into space. I dropped about ten feet, then the risers snapped onto the guy wire and I was off on a rapid ride down the wire. I was bouncing like a minnow on a fixed line until I rapidly stabilized and reached up to grab the risers, as I had been instructed. My relief at not having to fall three stories to the ground was rapidly overtaken by the realization that I was headed straight for the steel pole! Before I could voice my concern, my risers hit a stop in the wire, swinging me high in the air and stopping me short of impact. As I swung back down, two safety guys were at the ready to get me down. A few minutes later, I was back at the base of the tower, ready to do it again.

Monday of the second week brought a new challenge. The PT runs were now 3.5 miles long and by the end of the week would be an even four. The tower jumps were nearly eight times higher! Much of the week was spent in a swing harness, also known as suspended agony. Another device to teach us about the dynamics of descending under a parachute canopy.

Along with more work on the 34-foot towers, the class got to do a drop from the 250-foot tower. This was to familiarize us with the feeling of free fall and descending under a nylon canopy. This was an essential exercise because the following Monday would see us putting on a parachute rig and jumping from a plane for the first time.

The third Monday had us feeling pretty good. The 4-mile run was a piece of cake and the training of the previous weeks made us feel untouchable. Our bodies had become like rocks. It is amazing what just fourteen days of heavy physical activity can do to a person. We were now ready for our first jump, bringing us even closer to the almost mystical status of "Army Airborne."

Some things you never forget. Sgt. Rucker, my first jump, and "413" are three. After 55 plus years, with vivid clarity, I still recall my first jump. We were packed into a Fairchild C 119, also known as a World War II Flying Boxcar. We would make what was called a Hollywood jump, just a main and reserve chute; no gear, no weapons. The cargo plane revved up and you could sense the fear and anxiety as it raced down the runway. The forward thrust pushed each trooper against the other. Suddenly, the pilot hit the brakes and the reverse thrust now had us leaning on the guy on the other side. As I looked across the plane to the men on the inboard side, their already pale visage had become leeched of any color at all. *We were trained to jump out of this thing and now we'll die on the runway.* The pilot circled and tried three times before we became airborne. We found out later that if the plane was not airborne by a certain point, he had to abort the take-off and go around.

Finally, we were up, up, and away. It was only a short flight. We received a six-minute warning and then went through the jump commands: stand up, hook up, stand in the door, and go. On my first jump, I was out the door without hesitation. Sent through the prop blast, my feet together and above my head, suddenly the chute opened, jerking my feet toward the earth. Then I was sailing peacefully to the ground. I thought to myself What the hell am I doing here? I made a two-point landing ... my feet and my head. Forget the PLF! Hit, shift, and rotate worked in training, but the practical application was another story.

I was glad to leave that aircraft. Given all the effort it took to get the old thing up, I did not want to try landing in it. We finished up with four more successful jumps. School was over. Our wings were presented to us in the drop zone after the last jump. With the wings came my orders for Special Forces Training Group, Fort Bragg, North Carolina.

9. *Special Forces Training*

All spruced up and looking sharp, I boarded the military bus headed for Smoke Bomb Hill, home of the Special Forces Training Group. Beads of sweat rolled off my face as I exited the bus. It was hot, but I think I had a bad case of nerves. I was directed to the orderly room where I presented my orders to the First Sargent.

"Hi, Phillips, welcome to the training group. Have you had lunch yet?"

"No, Sargent. I haven't." He gave me directions to the mess hall and said, "Tell the mess sergeant I said to feed you."

There had been a lot of talk in the past three weeks about Special Forces and the badass training. The stories conjured up from recruitment fliers were incredible. I believed most of them But not knowing any better, I believed most of them! Such was the one about the "gorilla pit." Supposedly, new trainees would be pushed into a large hole in the ground that was surrounded by opposing forces, and then they would have to fight their way out. The gorilla pit was so heavy on my mind when I arrived at the Fayetteville bus station, that I checked my bags, all except for one small "AWOL bag." I was sure that if I had to fight off half of the Special Forces group, I didn't want to be fumbling with luggage.

I had a nice meal but ate light because I was sure the gorilla pit was coming. Everyone seemed too nice, and I was waiting for the other shoe to drop. After lunch, I returned to the orderly room, had a chat with the commanding officer, and was told I was going to MOI.

"MOI? May I ask what that is?"

"Methods of Instruction. We will teach you how to instruct indigenous personnel. That will only be for three weeks. Then, communication, or comm school. Okay?"

"Yes, sir." Not that I had a choice.

All the horror stories seemed to be unfounded. Yes, we did hand-to-hand combat training and spent some time with inflatable boats, but no gorilla pit. We continued jumping from various planes. My favorite was the helicopter. I especially enjoyed the times when I could sit in the door with my feet hanging outside of the craft. How cool was that! Cool was not to be in my new vocabulary, and was soon replaced by indigenous, guerrilla warfare, incendiary, potassium, and the ten-dollar word "counterinsurgency," This was the very reason for the Special Forces. The training was a challenge with long days that proved to be both physically and mentally demanding. More than once, I thought I had bitten off more than I could chew. But, I was determined to continue and earn the right to wear the Green Beret.

We were expected to train the indigenous personnel in the conduct of unconventional warfare. Among the varied subjects were communications, radio generators, antennas, (this is the world before cell phones) demolitions, first aid, setting up drop zones and landing pads for helicopters, etc. Each day, I became more and more like a sponge. I studied at night when I could have gone to the PX for a beer. I became the student I had never been. I did not give two shits about algebra, but I could rattle off the muzzle velocity of the 4.2 mortar (960 feet per second with a maximum range of 6,000 yards.) I could recite the phonetic alphabet in the international Morse Code, and I was developing a knowledge of French. Here's the joke. This high school dropout was learning how to teach someone who did not even speak English.

My biggest challenge proved to be the communications class. I understood radios and generators, most of them no longer used today. My trouble was the Morse Code. Memorizing the alphabet was easy, but sending and receiving messages was a problem. Morse code is another language, with only dots and dashes that run together like music. I told the instructor that I thought I might be tone-deaf. He suggested I come to the evening practice session, but first, go to the PX and have two cans of beer to relax me. After several unsuccessful attempts, I was transferred to demolition.

Demolition did not require any rhyme or music, only memorizing different chemicals, compounds, and formulas to calculate the correct ratio of explosives to accomplish the desired result. One of the most intricate portions of the advanced demolition techniques dealt with the guerrillas behind enemy lines. We were schooled in such chilling strategies as mining a ditch beside the killing zone of an ambush to wipe out any troops still alive who tried to take cover. Timing devices were included so you could be long gone when things went "boom."

Upon completion of demo training, I removed the training group flash from my beret and replaced it with the full red flash that designated the 7th Group. I stood in front of the mirror, making sure the red flash was centered over my left eye. I smiled at myself. You made it, you son of a bitch, you made it. Military life continued. If we weren't learning, we were teaching.

Most of the senior noncoms were Korean War vets or had some mission training or experience in Laos or Cambodia. At that time, those missions were still classified. It was Friday morning when Sgt. Vic Tammy ended his survival class by demonstrating the technique for biting off the head of a snake. Brave and unforgettable! Sushi, before it became popular. The Red Cross, he announced, was having a blood drive at 1300 hours. Anyone donating blood would be excused for the rest of the afternoon and could get a jump start on the weekend. I had no plans for that weekend, but I thought giving blood was a good thing to do.

After lunch, I shuffled into the line along with about 200 other guys who were anxious to chill out for the weekend. Red Cross volunteers had stations set up to process the donor's information. A lady in a neatly starched striped dress called, "Next."

I stepped forward and took a seat. Peering over her dark-rimmed glasses, she asked for my name, rank, and company.

"Phillips, PFC, Company A, 7th Special Forces." She prepared the paperwork and pricked my finger. I flinched and she apologized. I said, "It's okay I was just being a baby." She milked down my middle finger as we both watched a drop of blood falling to the solution in the test tube. She gathered the papers along with an empty blood bag and tubing.

"Come, let me take the baby to a cot."

I noticed an accent. "Germany?" I inquired.

"No, but close." She smiled and handed me over to another Red Cross lady.

"What's close to Germany?"

"I'll see you later," she said, obviously not looking for conversation.

One pint lighter, I was escorted to the recovery area for juice. From behind me, I heard, "How did the baby do?" I turned at the near German accent.

"Oh, the baby did fine." I noticed her clear, pale, sun-deprived complexion, which contrasted with her deep red puffy lips. She offered a tray of cookies and juice.

"You work both ends of this program?"

"Yes, I do everything."

In a short conversation, I learned she was from Holland and had a teenage daughter. Before I finished the juice and cookies, I was invited to Sunday dinner. I declined the offer, explaining my lack of transportation.

"Not a problem. I'll pick you up when I pick up Jack."

"Who's Jack?"

"My daughter's boyfriend. He comes every Saturday and Sunday."

"How old is your daughter?"

"Sixteen."

Sarcastically I said, "You're inviting a stranger to your home? You don't even know me."

"Lawrence Phillips, Company A, 7th Special Forces group. You are 22 years old. I'll be in the orderly room at 1030."

"By the way, I am Alma, Alma Becker."

"How does Mr. Becker feel about your bringing home strangers?"

"It's Master Sargent Becker, and he's got a soft spot for guys when they live on base. We met in Holland during the war where both of us went a long time with little food. So that's... what you call it? What do you say? Our thing? The Sargent is long retired, but he still works at the base supply."

"I look forward to meeting Sargent Becker."

***

I was dressed in neatly pressed slacks and a collared, short-sleeved shirt. As I headed for the orderly room, a short toot from a '59 green Cadillac alerted me to my ride. There sat Jack, Eleanor, and Mrs. Becker; all with cheery "good mornings." It was a short ride to the modest frame home that sat on sandy soil with tall pines that painted shadows on the front yard. Standing in the doorway, Sargent Becker gave the impression that at one time he may have stood taller. His bushy gray hair and bristling brows gave witness to a full and challenging life. He appeared to be much older than his wife.

Sunday dinner was enjoyable. There was comfortable small talk and afterward, board games. Part of the small talk included how their property line butted up against the Fort Bragg property. Between them was just a fire break, nothing more than a dirt road that continued around the base to give emergency vehicles access. Sargent Becker, now Donald, could drive to work and never go out on a public road or pass through a gate. Access to the base was open and free-flowing then.

The invites to their home continued until one late Saturday night, I was given the keys to the Caddy. I could return it when I came to Sunday dinner.

After a time, I noted a lingering handshake or a casual brush on the shoulder from Alma. This escalated to casual footsie, accompanied by a soft smile. One evening, while helping clean up in the kitchen, she asked if I ever get away early. When I responded that sometimes classes break early, she suggested that I call her next time and she would make lunch.

By the time I got back to the barracks, my mind was spinning with fanciful ideas. *Could she just be overly friendly? Could I be reading too much into an invitation to lunch?* I decided there was only one way to find out.

A few days later, class ended at 1100 and would not reconvene until 1330. My phone call was answered with enthusiasm and when her welcoming embrace became an extended kiss, my suspicions were confirmed.

I must admit that the intrigue of being off base with a married woman had my heart beating like a jackhammer. This was my "Mrs. Robinson" moment. As she led me into the living room, I took in the short skirt, the halter top covering her bra-less breasts, and the high heels that added to the provocative sway of her hips. She knew she had my full attention as she stopped in the center of the living room and slowly turned so that I could appreciate all her attributes. Although ten years older than me, she was vibrant. While not beautiful in the classical sense, her clear blue eyes, full lips, and shoulder-length auburn hair could still make heads turn. And her body had a maturity that was in stark contrast to my experiences with girls my age. She had a roundness and enticing softness that drew me to her.

She extended her hand palm up, curling her fingers to beckon me to her. I responded, my clumsy calloused hand joining the supple softness of hers. "Let's sit a while before lunch."

She took the center seat of the sofa, as I gently sat next to her. She placed her hand in mine and said, "I'm so glad you could stop by."

I countered with, "To be honest, I was a little nervous.

"Oh?" she said "Don't be nervous. This will be our secret," as she patted my thigh in a reassuring gesture.

She continued to slide her hand across my leg. I turned halfway to come face-to-face, as the massaging hand moved to the inside of my thigh. Our glances locked as she broke into a mischievous smile and the short skirt became shorter. My eyes scanned the mountains pushing through the halter, and the valley between her soft milky thighs, then back to her face. She tilted to one side, with a nod as if to say, go ahead, you can touch me. As I placed my hand on her bare knee, she slid hers to my groin. I worked my way up her leg as our mouths met. The dueling tongues worked their way to ears and necks. I slipped back resting my head on the armrest. Alma extended her arms and placed her hands on either side of my head, exposing the breast that had worked free from her halter. I said "Aah" approvingly, as she chuckled lowering the tips into my flushed face.

She rolled off the couch, pushing the coffee table back. I started to join her on the floor when she purred, "No, no, wait. Relax, we don't have enough time to finish properly." I was sure I was seconds from finishing when she said, "Save it for me. It will be better next time."

I could feel the dampness in my pants and an ache in my stomach, as I drove back to the barracks. "Better next time" kept rolling over in my head. How could it get better? Better and properly? What could she do to make it better? Once again, everything is not learned in the classroom.

"Lunch" with Alma became more frequent, less rushed, and more satisfying for both of us. Occasionally we would even have lunch.

***

The second week in May 1963, the First Sergeant came out to the morning formation. He went down the line, "You, you, you," until he had selected thirty men. He sounded urgent and appeared to analyze each one of us. Finally, he spoke.

"You men are going on summer vacation to Fort Lee, Virginia. You'll be gone until the end of July. Have your bags packed and be ready by 0700."

We all had questions. Could we take civvies? Is this some kind of a training mission? Will we have any free time? Was this a school? By the time we were scheduled to leave, most of our questions had been answered.

The need for a new combat boot design had been generated by the returning Special Forces troops who had stepped on Punji sticks. Punjis were sharpened bamboo sticks, sometimes soaked in animal or human feces, then planted where our men or the guerrilla forces would step on them. They were sharp enough to penetrate the soles of the current boots, so an immediate order was issued to come up with something better. The Quartermaster was tasked to come up with a design that would protect from jungle moisture, be lightweight, and have soles that could withstand the penetration.

The boots we were to test were leather and canvas; leather over the foot, canvas up the sides, with drain holes in the arch. We were told the sole had flexible steel plates in them. We would test the boots, with full combat gear, every day on specially created tracks. "Everyday" turned out to be Monday through Friday.

We were introduced to the "Monday, Wednesday, Friday track" and then the "Tuesday, Thursday trail." The trail traversed through the woods and hills with obstacles to climb, designed to test the cleats for traction. The track was just wide enough for two men to walk side-by-side. It was a combination of surfaces, mostly rough, ranging from sandpaper to broken glass embedded in concrete. The track was about one-third of a mile long and included troughs with chemical-infused water. Our mileage would be logged by a lieutenant and a sergeant from the Quartermaster Corps.

After seeing the course, we settled in our new quarters. After lunch, we assembled for a medical checkup of our feet, were weighed, and issued our boots. And so it began, the track, the trail, and the trial...

***

On weekends, I would hitchhike home to New York, where I spent quite a bit of time with Carol. Despite my erratic, unsettled, adventurous traveling spirit she had hung on to my offer to marry her. Our relationship had progressed nicely and I had met her parents, Charlie and Dorothy, and her sister, Barbara. You know it's serious when you get to sit down with Mr. Caserta. Charlie was a typical old-time Italian father. Never a man was born good enough for his girls.

The Green Beret was as new to everyone else as it was to me. President Kennedy had recently ordered it as the new uniform for

Special Forces. It sparked questions from her friends and family. Are you seeing a Canadian? What country is he from? It was difficult to explain guerrilla warfare in a country called South Vietnam. Few people knew of it, or the buildup of Special Forces to fight the communist insurgents from the north.

What was not difficult to explain was the wedding plans. Yes, the wedding was on the horizon. A whirlwind romance, so it seemed to me. After all, I had been fully occupied in a variety of things Carol would neither approve of nor hear about if I could help it. She made all the plans and brought me up to date on the weekends. Before I knew it, the date was set, the church selected, and the dress purchased. Charlie and Dot were paying for everything. All I had to do was show up on July 20th.

Right. They may have been sure, but I was starting to have my doubts. How in the world could I support a wife on little more than $100 a month? I convinced myself that if I had my health and strength, I would persevere. ? I had great self-confidence and always met my challenges. Carol continued to make plans, which included an engagement party.

"How can we do that? I don't have a ring."

"No problem. Barbara has one she wants to give us. It's from her short-lived marriage to Ronald."

"I can't pay for it," I insisted.

"She said she wouldn't take anything for it."

Both the engagement and party happened. We accepted the ring from Barbara, with her blessing and instructions not to mention it again.

We went to check out the Regency Catering Facility in Jamaica. It was exceptionally large and glitzy. As she explained the plans, I became dry-mouthed as I saw the gathering dollar signs.

"How much is this place and what are your parents spending?"

"$10,000," she blurted out.

"Holy cow! How'd they get that much money?"

"Don't worry, my mother saves every penny."

"It's not fair that your family gives everything while my parents can't help out at all."

"Don't worry!"

"Please, don't tell me not to worry. It's just not right and I can't do anything, except show up on July 20th."

***

I requested leave for the wedding and a two-week honeymoon. "Denied!"

Denied? What do you mean denied?"

"All requests are denied until we finish this test. You have to complete 500 miles in the boots."

I cried, complained, and explained, "But Sarge, I'm getting married."

I was told to stop my pissing and moaning. "I'll call back to headquarters and see what they say."

Two days later, Fort Bragg decided that the Quartermaster alone had the authority to grant my leave. What they say goes. If the Quartermaster allows it, they will send up the leave papers. At that point, everything took two days. The Quartermaster's reply: "You can go to your wedding but only if you complete the 500 miles."

The captain in charge of the test came out to the track one day asking for me. "Phillips, do you know why your people were sent here for this test?" Before I could answer, "Because, you have the integrity to finish this job! Your group requested them, and your people will be wearing them. We believe you will give them one hell of a good test."

He stopped long enough to take a breath, "Here's the deal. See how many more turns on the track you need to make 500 miles. I don't care if you walk double-time or run full speed day and night. Just give me 500 miles and you can have your wedding and your honeymoon."

"Thank you, sir! You've got a deal." It was determined that I had 75 miles more to complete my 500. That meant 225 laps, in addition to the regular count. About 3.75 extra miles per day for 20 days. Each day I grew to the challenge, counting the days and the miles needed to reach the 500-mile mark.

At first, the other 29 men on the detail thought it strange for me to keep walking on my time off, through lunch, and after quitting time. Soon they all knew the reason and cheered me on. Some of the guys were making bets on whether I would complete the "Phillips 500" in time. Finally, I crossed the finish line with one day to spare. The southern sun had generated perspiration that could have been measured in quarts. I was presenting myself, the bridegroom in the best possible physical condition, not an ounce of fat or flab anywhere, even my muscles had muscles.

10. The Wedding

July 20, 1963, 3:50 p.m. and the sky was threatening rain. Inside, my brother Paul stood by my side, as a million butterflies thundered inside my belly. The soft organ music and the aroma of fresh flowers served as the backdrop as the procession began. Preceded by the ushers and bridesmaids, the bride appeared. As she paused at the back of the church on her father's arm, a nervous smile crinkled the corners of her eyes. When they reached the altar, Charlie raised his daughter's veil, kissed her lightly, and gestured for me to take his place. Then, every one of those butterflies went still. It was at that moment I realized this was the real deal. No walking away, no flying away, no leaving town. Today I become a responsible adult.

The Regency House did a great job. The cocktail hour was held in a room with ceiling to floor velvet curtains. It was illuminated by crystal chandeliers with hundreds of glittering pendants. The 200 plus guests were served hors d'oeuvres by a wait staff neatly attired in a black vest, bow tie, and white gloves. The wedding party and our parents were ushered into a large lounge area to pose for photos. "Turn this way, hold your head up, look down, step to your left, best man gives the ring to the groom, look surprised, everyone smile." Then came the grand entrance, "Lineup, please. First the parents, then the bridesmaids and groomsmen, the maid of honor and the best man." Each one was announced by name, and then, like a circus ring master minus the top hat.

"Ladieeees and Gentlllemen! Appearing for the first time as man and wife, Mr. & Mrs. Lawrence Phillips."

After the first dance, when the applause ended, we took our seats behind the four-tiered wedding cake. The formalities were over, except for the cutting of the cake and tossing the bride's bouquet. We made the customary rounds, thanking all the guests for attending. Several times during the festivities, Carol tried to have a conversation with me, but we were continuously interrupted. Finally, in exasperation, "Forget about it. I'll tell you later."

The evening drew to a close and we were whisked off in the limousine to her parents' house where we changed clothing. We then piled into her car with our luggage, the satin bag stuffed with cash gifts, and a bottle of champagne. Raindrops danced on the windshield as I drove the 55 Chevy west on Belt Parkway toward Brooklyn and a newly built motel. We pulled under the portico, I checked in at the desk and then moved to the parking spot in front of our room. We dashed to our room to avoid a soaking.

"I've been trying to get you in a motel for quite a while." I quipped, trying to allay Carol's obvious nervousness.

"I'm afraid you are not going to be very happy with me."

"Oh, yes I will," I said, dropping our bag on the floor and moving to take her in my arms.

"I, I got a surprise this morning," she murmured.

"What kind of surprise?"

"My friend."

"Who?"

"You know, my friend."

I started to ask again and then it hit me "Oh, that's not friendly."

"I know, but I can't do anything about it. I've been trying to tell you all night." Plopping down on the edge of the bed she said, "I'm sorry."

OK, Phillips. Here is where you act like an adult. This calls for patience, understanding, and abstinence... abstinence? "Honey, I'm sorry, too. But this is the first day of the rest of our lives. We'll have many nights to make love. Why don't we get comfortable and then we will have some champagne."

She was lovely in her white peignoir set which flowed softly from her shoulders, brushing the floor as she crossed the room toward me. I rose quickly to meet her, in nothing more than my government-issued boxer shorts. I could sense her nervousness as I embraced her. After a lingering kiss, she shared with me that she felt clumsy and that it just did not feel right.

In an attempt to make her feel more comfortable, I called on my limited and newfound maturity, suggesting we sit and talk about it.

After several hours of conversation, and with the aid of the champagne, I learned that my bride had been raised to believe that sex before marriage would put her soul in a cylinder and shoot it straight to hell. She had also been taught that sex was dirty and that enjoying it would label her a bad girl. It was clear that she had not been given any reason to look forward to the sex act before or after marriage. I could foresee long hours of talk therapy and massage. Unfortunately, our long periods of separation would be a further complication. A combination of the day's activities, the excitement of the evening, and the champagne led to our falling asleep in each other's arms.

After breakfast at a local diner, we headed to Atlantic City and the Virginian Motel, the first stop on our official honeymoon. This was before casinos, when walking on the boardwalk was a summer pastime, with pedicabs, amusements, and benches overlooking the beach. The steel pier was a carnival that jutted out over the breaking surf. At the end was a tower where a horse would climb to the top and dive into the surf.

On the third day, as we passed the pay phone, Carol asked if I had any change so that she could call her mom.

"Everything okay?" I asked as she replaced the receiver.

"Yes, everything is fine. She wanted to know if I felt married." she looked at me with a sad face and shrugged. "I told her, no."

I put my arm around her shoulders. "We drive to the Poconos tomorrow, and I think by that time, we should be ready to start our honeymoon."

Upon arrival at the honeymoon resort where we had reserved a cabin, we surveyed the grounds and the dining room, making ourselves familiar with the area. The heat and humidity were nearly unbearable and the cabin was no cooler. As we pulled back the drapes, a flood of light revealed a vaulted ceiling with beams sectioning off the white popcorn textured paint job. The quilted gray satin spread contrasted against the deeper gray shag carpet. The easy chair was cornered with a goose-neck pole lamp for reading. Who reads on their honeymoon? The dark wood paneling absorbed most of the light. The bathroom, however, was bright white and sterile looking. There was an oversized porcelain tub with a six-inch ledge all around.

We had a few hours before the evening meal, so we decided to freshen up; silently communicating that it was time to consummate our marriage. Respecting her modesty, we took turns in the shower. We returned to the bedroom; each having doused ourselves with talcum powder. What resulted was a memorable afternoon and not just for the obvious reason. The lack of air conditioning caused the talcum powder and perspiration to turn into a white paste; both unattractive and uncomfortable! Then, at the most inopportune time, I experienced a horrendous muscle spasm in my leg. A result of the 500-mile walk?. I cringed with pain, my body arched, and when my gyrations ended, I was a white, sticky mass perched on the edge of the bed trying to catch my breath. Carol thought I was having a stroke or heart attack. Later she would share, "I thought I was going to be a widow and still a virgin."

The rest of the week was spent enjoying the amenities and taking long walks (as if I had not walked enough). Our evenings were candlelit, exploring each other's sexuality. I was still running to first base arriving too soon. Carol was left wondering what happened. We expected marriage would present problems and obstacles. This was our first.

11. A Walk in the Woods

With both our honeymoon and my leave at an end, I returned to Fort Bragg and Carol returned to her job at the insurance company. Everything returned to normal, whatever that was.

One evening I was called to the orderly room for a phone call, a summons normally reserved for emergencies. "Hello?" I knew in an instant it was Alma.

"How was Virginia and the wedding? We want to hear all about it. Come to dinner Sunday."

Hesitating, "I...I..."

"I'll pick you up at 1030. See you Sunday. Bye."

I replaced the receiver as Sgt. Bing queried "The Cadillac lady, Phillips?"

"How do you know about her?"

"Everybody knows."

"You don't understand. She's married with a family. We're friends"

"Sure, if you say so."

Sunday dinner was just Alma, Don, and me. The boyfriend, Jack, had been discharged and had returned home, taking Eleanor with him. Alma and I picked up where we had left off. It was hard to believe that her husband could be in the next room, clueless, while another man was kissing and fondling his wife. He could have walked in on us without warning. Those kinds of surprises make national headlines, *"Newlywed found shot to death at Fort Bragg."* The thought of being exposed or becoming the latest scandal scared me to death, but still, I did little to resist. Every short hair stood at attention, every skin cell tingled, every neuron fired. I motioned to the next room, and she gave me a one-shoulder shrug. Don seemed to be sleeping in his easy chair while Alma and I pretended to play cards.

***

Smoke Bomb Hill was a beehive of activity. After PT and chow, there was morning formation. When that broke, everyone went to their designated area for their activities of the day. Many times, it was a class given by one of the noncoms. Basic Special Forces A-Team consisted of twelve men, two of each specialty (operations, intelligence, weapons, communications, demolition, and medical). Cross-training was ongoing. The concept was that each team member would be trained in another specialty. I can say now that I loved those days, being exposed to learning new things every day. It was like ripping open the top of my head and filling it with gallons of liquid smarts. Those Dominican sisters had been wrong. I was teachable.

The A-Teams work and train together with the intent of being deployed as a cohesive unit. Some teams were in mission training that included the language and customs of the indigenous personnel they would meet, if and when deployed. There were many teams in "mission training." Of course, the content of those sessions was classified. This gave birth to the cliche "If I tell you, I'll have to kill you." Everything was on a need-to-know basis. My curiosity was peaked when I heard "Laos, Cambodia and Vietnam" without an inkling of where in the world they were. I had suspected a buildup was going on someplace and my suspicions were confirmed when I was told my team would be spending mornings at the language lab.

"What the hell is the language lab?"

"Phillips, that's a classroom where you learn another language like French or Vietnamese."

"Hey, Sarge, I'm from New York I have enough trouble with English."

"Roger that, y'all."

A short history lesson followed. South Vietnam's President Ngo Dinh Diem came to power in 1955 when Vietnam separated into North and South. He was deposed and assassinated during the 1963 military coup led by General Duong Van Minh. I was not privy to the politics and policies of the State Department, and in all honesty, I would not have understood anyway.

I decided to concentrate on the French taught by a Vietnamese refugee There was no grammar or spelling, only spoken words and phrases designed to gather information. Such as, how many men and what kind of weapons, road conditions, and any activity in the area. I called it operational French.

With the conclusion of the language lab, my team was selected for a detail that did not involve any schooling. It was more in line with the boot testing assignment.

This time it would be thirty days in a North Carolina national forest surviving on newly adopted rations that had been designed for long-range patrols. Orientation took place at a mountain lodge, taken over by the Army as a headquarters for the month of testing. Instructions were for each half team to be dropped off with maps marked with rallying points where they would meet every few days. This was all done with full battle gear to simulate combat under jungle conditions. Every ten days, we would return to the lodge and undergo a quick physical, including blood tests. Each team would then receive a ten-day supply of different rations. The officer conducting the test made it clear that we were to eat the designated amounts.

We were introduced to the three different rations. One was the conventional C rations, first issued in 1939. That ten-day supply weighed a ton. Number two was a lightweight fruit bar packed in foil, no bigger than a candy bar. Some of them were chocolate coated. The third was a powdered substance that was to be mixed with water. We nicknamed it 'Metrecal' after a diet drink being marketed at that time.

Our operations specialist, Sergeant Stone, had a full face and was slightly balding. He was extremely proud of his home state of Tennessee. In the woods, he was "Stony." Our intelligence man was James Simpson (Jimbo), a black man from the Bronx. Specialist Gallo was our radio operator, a nice Italian boy from Brooklyn. Gallo could bench press over 300 pounds. Bernard Fitz-Alan, "Fitzy" for short, was our weapons specialist. He was always a gentleman, even in the woods. Dale Hudson, a smooth, soft-spoken, young man from Dallas, was our medic. He constantly practiced tying surgical knots, hoping he never needed to use them. Oh yeah, I was "Boom."

"Your first ten days will be C rations. You might want to repackage them to fit in your rucksacks. Load up. The three-quarter will drop you at you're first starting point."

We loaded the cases into the truck and jumped in behind them. By the time we rolled to a stop, we had repacked the larger boxes and emptied some of the containers into the outer pockets of our rucksacks. 0900 hours on the dirt road, the six of us watched the pickup truck drive away. As Stony navigated with map and compass, the rest of the team pondered what to do with the rations that wouldn't fit in our rucksacks.

"Pack what you can. Carry the rest," was Stony's order. More bad news! "Gather around. This is Dog's Back Mountain. There's a road at the top but our only way is up through the woods."

"Holy shit, it must be 80 degrees and we still have three cases of C rations to drag along behind us."

"Phillips, I know you can do it!"

"Sure, Stony, but it may take us ten days."

"Nope, that's only the start. Once we reach the road, we have at least eight more days to go. Here's the plan. Three men lead, three men carry one case each. When we break, we switch. The three leaders carry, that way we all share the load."

Not to sound like a crybaby with my "holy shit" and 80 degrees comment, I volunteered to carry the first stretch. Only fifteen minutes had passed, and it became obvious why it was called

Dog's Back Mountain. The brush was as thick as the hair on a dog. High noon, not even halfway up the hill, Stony called a halt.

"Here is my new revised plan. Let's bury three cases someplace and mark the grave. If we have to recover them, we can send two men back with empty rucksacks. Everyone agreed?"

Airborne! Agreed!

"Okay, this meeting and this conversation never happened."

"Roger that."

"I'll shoot an azimuth from the road. Gallo. mark the trail with foil wrappers from the ration packs. Dusty and Fitz, break out your entrenching tools and start digging."

The trees offered some shade but little comfort for digging and hiking. The sweat chafed my groin and underarms, and my vision was blurred by the droplets of perspiration hanging from my eyelids. Gnats or some other of God's creation found comfort in my ears, just annoying the hell out of me. I continued to climb up the hill, all the time thinking how I was going to be a trained killer in a Green Beret. But today, this woolly green rug was just too hot, the food too heavy, and the crotch too raw. Thank God for foot powder, it works anywhere. Testing boots, testing food, most of all testing me by pushing me to my limits. I know, I asked for it and I will never give up. Whenever it is over, I'll still be standing tall and proud (maybe not too tall).

"1700. Let's make camp on the side of the road. Far enough to be out of sight should anyone come along. Pitch your jungle hammock to stay off the ground."

Jungle hammocks were used in place of, or in conjunction with, sleeping bags. We strung our hammocks between two trees, three to four feet above the ground, safe from small animals and the moisture. We all gathered around a few fallen trees and had dinner. Wondering if the C rations would be just as heavy on the inside as they were on the outside.

We buried our garbage and the rest of our C rations, desserts, cigarettes, and anything else we didn't want to carry. The collective thinking was that if we ran out of food, we would live off the land; leaves, berries, trapped animals, whatever target presented itself in the next nine days. We all carried AR 15's and .45

automatics. Some of us had ammunition to fight off some large game (but that was unofficial.) Ten days later we dragged ourselves back into the lodge. We were afforded hot showers before our physicals. The medics certainly did not want to touch anybody with ten days of crotch rot. We received a thorough inspection and a new supply of powder and salt tablets.

Stony called the team together. "Our next challenge is the fruit bar. Ten days, three bars a day, definitely a lighter load. We move out at 0600. Find a place to sleep. I want to cover as much ground as we can before the sun comes up."

The first day, the first bar, the first gag. A muffled gagging sound that mimicked, "holy shit" again. Everyone looked at me. I was more verbal, but I couldn't get the sticky, slimy, crunchy, sweet medicine-tasting bar out of the way of my vocal cords.

C rations were starting to look better. The next ten days' terrain was not as challenging as the first ten. Our load was lighter and the trails less difficult. Gallo and I bonded as we walked the mountain ridge. He spoke of his Italian roots and his uncles who had promised him a job when he got home. He wasn't sure what they did for a living. The only thing I knew about Italian heritage, I had learned from Dominic's Pizza and Muttsy (short for mozzarella).

First name, Joe, he lived around the corner, across from the Cox's Army. Muttsy's family was totally old country Italian. The household included grandpa, who spoke wine, but no English, mother, aunt, and some other children. The basement was where you could find grandpa and three or four barrels of wine cradled in the dugout under the front porch. Grandpa was liked by all of us. He always had a pat on the head and a few words for each of us.

Our little walk down memory lane helped to ease the pain and cleanse our palates. God, those fruit bars sucked. Sorry, no nice way to say it.

Our last ten days we survived on the "Metrecal." God only knew who made them. They were terrible! Even if you could carry two canteens, it still would not last ten days. So, the challenge was to meet our objectives on time and find water along the way. As we moved forward, we found some slippery rocks. That didn't mean much to a city kid like me, but the country boys knew it meant water was uphill. So, we climbed upstream, slipping and sliding on the algae-covered rocks. Calling them "snot rocks."

At the end of our 30 days, we returned to Fort Bragg and were rewarded with a 72-hour pass. Much needed and well-deserved. Jimbo and I caught a hop at Pope Air Force Base to Maguire Airbase in New Jersey next to Fort Dix. Living in barracks causes men to bond with no effort on their part. The size of the barracks put us in intimate contact with each other, and the latrine, with seven or eight commodes in a row and no modesty panels, was the ultimate stripping of all pretenses. All your gastrointestinal discomfort and sound effects were shared.

So, I should not have been surprised when Jimbo asked as we sat in the web belt seats of the otherwise empty cargo plane, "Did you shit yourself?"

"Of course not!"

A few minutes later he asked again, "Phillips, you shit?"

When I turned to answer him, he said "Christ, it's your breath. I mean, it smells like shit. What did you eat?"

"I ate the same crap you ate for 30 days."

Before we had touched down in New Jersey, I had come to the full and panicked realization that I had a problem. Each time I belched or passed wind; a noxious odor formed a cloud around me. How would I greet my new bride and in-laws? I called home!

Carol, remember our vows, better or worse? This may be the worse and I don't know for how long."

The weekend passed with an abundance of breath mints, chewing gum, and Listerine.

12. Return to Fort Bragg

When I received orders to report to the engineering school at Ft. Belvoir, Virginia. *Are they crazy?* I didn't even finish high school, I can't even spell 'engineer.' The formal title was the NCO Combat Construction Course. It would be fourteen weeks, eight hours a day, Monday through Friday. Once again, I was being prepped for a buildup in Vietnam or some other undisclosed location. Like every other challenge, I would give it my best. Failure was not an option.

The school was 260 hours of nonstop information, new experiences, and challenges. Each day I gained a new appreciation for the value of education. About a third of the way through the course, I was convinced civil engineering could have been for me. I was overwhelmed by the exposure to formulas for moving earth, calculating the capacity of dump trucks, travel time to clear a roadway, the swing time of cranes, and shelter building. The information was endless, and I loved it. Every block of instruction exposed me to tools and equipment I had never seen or heard of. Not in a cocky way, but I was feeling good about myself.

The course completed, a certificate in hand, I proudly returned to Fort Bragg. My next block of instruction was learning how to rappel from a tower. Going over the edge on a rope was nerve-racking, depending solely on the belay man should you fall. He alone controlled your descent. By the third time, I was enjoying it. My confidence in my fellow team members was cemented when they tied me in a litter and lowered it over the edge.

One morning, I was approached by the First Sargent about building a repelling tower for the Special Warfare Center demonstration area. I started to explain that I was a pole lineman in my first enlistment. He acknowledged that he had looked at my records. My engineering course was why he had approached me. It was agreed I would create a bill of materials and get back to him. We checked out the site to be used, ordered six large telephone poles and the necessary lumber to secure them, and added a wall and deck with safety rails and a ladder. Within two weeks, the tower stretched sixty-foot six inches above the ground and was painted olive drab. I was the first to rappel. At the base were General Yarborough and Colonel Evans-Smith, Special Warfare Commander and Seventh Group Commander, respectively. I must have made an impression on them because a week later I was called to group headquarters and offered a position as the commander's aid/driver. Since such positions were generally a path to promotion, it took no time at all for me to agree. I was interviewed by Evans-Smith. He was well built, prematurely gray, and very pleasant. After the interview, I asked, "Sir, this may be a little out of line, but may I ask why I was selected for this position?"

"Phillips, to be honest, I was impressed with the rappelling tower last week. Not only that, but I noticed your name on several letters I endorsed from the General's office when you were selected as his orderly. You completed two difficult tasks, the boots at Fort Lee and the rations in North Carolina. You are to be commended on both of those. It is quite clear that you could represent this office to my satisfaction, and I expect that you will."

"Thank you, sir. I will not disappoint you."

This new assignment came with a few perks. I could jump the chow line and hang out looking busy while doing nothing, as long as the Jeep looked good. I befriended an artist GI and conned him into painting the cover for the spare tire which was mounted on the back of the Jeep. The result was more professional than I had ever expected. The words "Commanding Officer 7th Special Forces Group" encircled the green beret with the Seventh red flash. He also made a front license plate that displayed the Silver Eagle, usually reserved for general grade officers. I could travel anywhere in that vehicle, within reason, and no one would question me.

***

I was at Fort Bragg when John F. Kennedy was assassinated. It was a Friday afternoon when I noticed troops rushing into the Colonel's office, totally out of protocol. No one entered before knocking, and never without an appointment. I could feel the excitement and tension in the air as everyone huddled around the TV. Something was very wrong. Gradually, the info filtered back to within my hearing. "Oh my God, someone shot the President."

The next few days were full of speculation and anticipation. A Special Forces honor guard was selected from a hastily assembled group of volunteers. I was not selected, but I would have been so proud to have been able to stand guard in the Rotunda. It became clear that the criteria for selection included height, build, and a combination of hash marks and campaign ribbons. The selected were a group of seasoned professionals wearing the headgear that JFK had specifically authorized for Special Forces soldiers. They performed with honor and distinction.

***

As our training continued, two new programs were introduced on the hill. First was High Altitude Low Opening, (HALO) military skydiving and the other, which I longed to try (thrill seeker that I was) was Sky Hook. This is how an evacuee is snatched off the ground by a fixed-wing aircraft. Equipped with a forked apparatus, it was designed to catch a helium balloon tethered to the subject's harness. At this point, he would be swept off the ground at over a hundred miles per hour. Whoopee!

***

On the home front, Carol was pregnant and due mid-May. My last trip home had been Labor Day (no pun intended) making it easy to pinpoint conception. My trips home were infrequent because New York was outside of the legal area for a basic 48-hour pass. Plus, hitchhiking would take more time than I had, and even driving was at least 12 hours each way. Even today, with the completion of US 95, it still takes that long.

A combination of our physical separation, pregnancy, and living with her parents caused Carol's nesting instincts to kick in. She was longing for a home of her own. However, when I suggested she move to Fort Bragg, she became upset. Neither living on post nor off-post appealed to her. She was more attached to her family than I had realized.

It soon became clear, she expected me to be discharged and come home to find a job. Try as I might to explain that I would have six years in toward retirement, or how I expounded on the benefits of free medical, shopping at the commissary, longevity promotional increases, none of this could penetrate. She wanted her vision of the American dream, the house with a white picket fence, etc., etc. I had about 18 months before a decision must be made.

I continued to volunteer for deployment, but somehow mission teams evaded me. At that time, teams received per diem, jump pay, and demo pay. It was an opportunity to save some money because you had no place to spend it. Most of the men selected were veterans of the Korean conflict or had been deployed and returned with invaluable experience. I continued to make known to the proper individuals, my sincere and overwhelming desire to join the next mission team. With everything being so classified, I could not ask why I wasn't picked or even if there were any teams in training. In time, it became a more conventional operation, with all branches taking part.

***

One bright, sunny afternoon, having just returned from lunch, I was summoned into the adjutant's office.

"Sit down, Phillips. I may have a job for you."

"Yes, sir. What can I do for you?"

"Are you tired; did you get a good night's sleep?"

"No, sir and yes, sir"

"You may have to work late."

"Yes, sir," finally. "What's up?"

"One of our men, Sgt. Jackson, is dying on the island of Okinawa We are tasked with getting his wife there, asap. The doctors seem to think her presence will give him the will to live." *How unusual, to transport a dependent to a bedside halfway around the world.* My confusion must have shown on my face.

Capt. Ambrose said softly "Phillips, it's important to keep him alive and I'm not going to say another word. Understood?"

"Loud and clear, sir" I assumed Sgt. Jackson must have had some classified information that they didn't want to go to the grave with him.

"Report to the motor pool at 1600 to pick up a staff car. It'll be ready to go with a full tank of gas."

Now the smart ass comes out, "Hey, even a full tank won't get me to Okinawa." Realizing in all the secrecy he had not told me where I was to take Mrs. Jackson, he placed both hands firmly on his desk and stared down. Shaking his head back and forth, and acknowledging the oversight with a broad smile, "You're right, but it will get you to the Charlotte airport. That's where you'll be taking Mrs. Jackson to meet her flight."

"Roger that, I'll get a road map" He interrupted, I'll have it all laid out for you when you return at 1600. All you have to do is drive. Now go."

When I returned, I was introduced to Mrs. North, a close friend of Mrs. Jackson, who would be traveling with us. "Mrs. Jackson will be arriving shortly with Chaplain Cooley. Here is a map, should you need it to get back. The MP's will provide an escort from here to Route 74 where the State Police will pick you up in Rockingham and escort you to the terminal."

During the trip, the two ladies reflected in the rear-view mirror were having a private conversation; one comforting the other. The escort was done in a relay with one car waiting, lights flashing as the current escort U-turned and returned to his regular duties.

As we approached the final trooper, he flagged me down.

"Listen! This is the last leg of the trip. Follow me and stay close. I'll take you right up to the terminal and get you all inside. Be safe, stay close." He looked at his watch, "Let's go."

Almost at once, I understood his "stay close" direction. He surely was pushing the ponies. The rural setting of a farm and a small crossroad with a general store passed as quickly as the short blast from the siren. I activated my emergency flashers, hoping that would show my association with the red "bubble gum machine" in front of me. Intersections became more frequent as the rush-hour traffic built up. As we pushed through the suburban streets most vehicles yielded to the red lights. However, the pedestrian traffic concerned me more. There were too many adults and children still in the streets, mothers with baby carriages scurrying home as the sun was setting. The one thing Ambrose had not thought of was a pair of sunglasses. Suddenly, the brake lights in front of me glared and, just as abruptly, I smashed the brake pedal to the floor. The ladies lunged forward, I veered right and hit the gas and was a car length behind the trooper. Apologizing to the ladies, "Sorry, ladies. I didn't see that coming." Two hours and 40 minutes later we pulled up to the terminal, with 20 minutes to spare. Mrs. North and I waited at the gate until Mrs. Jackson was off the ground.

After coffee and a trip to the facilities, "Mrs. North, I don't think we will get back as fast as we got here."

With a nod and a big smile, she said, "I hope not," and she slid into the passenger seat.

***

"Hey, Sgt. Stone, what are you doing here?" I asked as we both entered the headquarters building.

"The Colonel has a project for me."

"I hope it's not more ration testing."

"God forbid."

When Stony and the Colonel came out of his office, "Phillips, get the Jeep. You're coming with us. Head out to the drop zones."

As we got underway, the Colonel started to explain his project. "Phillips, listen up. I want you involved in this. You and Sgt. Stone will be building a couple of horse stalls for the Braxton Bragg Hunt Club." He continued to explain there was no budget for the job and we would need to arrange for some salvaged material. We were not to broadcast it.

We arranged to meet at 1630 the following day, in front of the orderly room. Exactly on time, he showed up with a 2-½ ton truck and some hand tools.

"We're going to the main post. There are some bleachers to disassemble that we can use for our project."

When he pulled up to the far end of the 82nd Airborne Division parade ground, I began to question if this was on the up and up.

"Don't ask," Stony read my mind. "Ditch the beanie!"

That confirmed it. I removed the beret and moved more quickly. This was my first "midnight requisition."

The construction was completed without a hitch and the Colonel presented us with a three-day pass and a letter of commendation, cleverly worded as a civic action project with little or no supervision. There was no word of salvaged material. Years later I heard of Special Forces being trained to ride and use horses as pack animals. The whole deal must have been classified. The Braxton Bragg Hunt Club was a cover and I had no "need to know."

What I did know was the adult education center was offering evening classes in preparation for the GED. I decided that if I ever acquiesced to Carol's wishes, I would need it to get a job and a GED would help. What I knew now was that I wasn't as dumb as I thought. However, my composition, spelling, and sentence structure were atrocious and needed help (some things never change).

***

Joe Cox married Stephanie (one of the Lee sisters) who lived next door to Carol. Lifetime friends, they shared everything, including their first pregnancies. Joe struggled both to gain and keep employment. His lack of education worked against him. Auto mechanic, body and fender work, and painting was his specialty; until he had to read a label or directions on a can. The frustration of all this drove him to start using drugs as an escape.

In addition to his obligations as a husband and father, now he had to support his increasing habit. He returned to his roots as a con man, selling non-existent, allegedly stolen merchandise to people in the community. Once he had your money, he would disappear. The mark would be out the imaginary merchandise, and their cash and Joe was nowhere to be found. He still had a sincere and honest way about him. A skill he learned as a kid on the Boulevard when homemakers opened their hearts and purses to the curly-haired, skinny kid who looked like he needed a good meal.

His small army of victims, vowing to at least break his legs, was growing. It was becoming more difficult for him to traverse the streets without being recognized. Sooner or later one of his prey, or the police, would catch up with him. He hoped it would be the cops, and it was. Joe went away for a short time... a few times.

On the first of May 1964, Carol quit her job in anticipation of the delivery of our first child. Fourteen days later, Robert was born. Stephanie gave birth to Deborah soon after. Both women raised their babies with absentee fathers.

***

The dilemma of choosing Army versus civilian life continued. Both phone and face-to-face conversations consisted of discussions of apartments, their availability, and the cost. Of course, this led to the subject of available jobs, what they paid, and how we would be able to live. Charlie encouraged me to take the test for the city sanitation, which I refused over and over.

I did take advantage of the walk-in test for the city police department. I was slightly below the 5'8" height requirement. I strategically placed paper towels, folded over to three-quarters of an inch thickness, in between two pairs of white wool socks, hoping that would get me close enough to trick the watchful eye of the monitor at the height and weight station. I even slept on the floor the night before, having heard that helps to straighten the spine and could add a half-inch to my height. Eliminated at the first station! "REJECTED" was stamped on my application form and served to reinforce my argument that I should stay in the service. Too good for a garbage truck, not good enough for a police car.

***

As an infant, Robert suffered the pain and discomfort of colic. Carol and her mother would alternate two-hour shifts each night, holding and attending to him. When I came home on weekends, Dottie would stay up with him through the night, affording Carol and me as much time together as possible. Carol and her mother would hold the baby in front of them, slightly above their stomachs, changing arms as they paced the floor, day and night. As the baby became heavier, they started pushing the abdomen out to support him which created back strain.

Caring for the baby while multitasking with housework often left Carol in a housecoat splattered with coffee, formula, and baby vomit. The glow of the expectant mother soon faded. All her waking hours were devoted to a child whose lungs were working fine even if his stomach was not.

When it came to parenting, I was almost always excluded, as Dottie appeared to be the only one with the know-how. I rarely spent time helping or holding. Were they protecting the baby from me or me from the baby? I only had Saturday to visit, because Sunday I had to be back on the road. As the months went by, I accepted my role of simply staying out of the way and thought I was handling it well. That was until…

One day my shortcomings were called to my attention. "You never say thank you for all the things my parents do for us. You have never thanked them for anything!"

"How absurd," I fired back. "That's not true."

"Yes, it is. Think about it."

"I don't have to think about it."

"Well, maybe you should."

And with that, she started to list everything for which I should be thankful. It sounded like a Chinese menu. I could select everything in column A and most of column B, as true. What an eye-opener! What had happened to me? Where was that little boy to whom my mother force-fed manners? I had been raised to say 'please and thank you,' never be seated when a lady was standing, hold the doors for women and the elderly. Did the Army do this to me? Had I become so mechanical, so regimented, so hard that there was no softness at all? In retrospect, I should have expressed my appreciation. Somehow, everything they did for me and my new family just seemed natural and I took it all for granted. How could I ever make it up to them? I could not just rattle off 35 thank yous for all of column A. That conversation set me back on my heels and I did some deep soul-searching on the long ride back to Fort Bragg.

***

I walked across the parade ground; a walk I had taken hundreds of times before. That day was different. I was still wrestling with the "thank you" conversation. I knew she was right, but what could I do? It was kind of after the fact.

The other thing racing around in my head was whether to be discharged or be a lifer. Make Carol happy or do what I believed was right for us? The vows reverberated in my head, love, honor... Then, "free medical" would flash by. It could be ours for life. Yep, that's it, I'm going to do what's right. I'll build our future in the Army. Already a well-trained soldier, nobody gets fired or laid off, this is pretty much a guaranteed job. I'll have six years toward a twenty-year retirement. That is an investment you should not just throw away.

"Good morning, Chaplin," as I entered the far end of the group headquarters. Capt. Cooley was exactly what you would expect from a man of the cloth. He was friendly, nonjudgmental, and easy to talk to. His office was furnished with the traditional desk and chairs, plus a conversation pit that included a sofa and two easy chairs.

Sauntering down the corridor, poking my head into certain offices. Greeting those I saw with a "good morning, sir, sergeant, or guys," depending on rank. As I arrived at the adjutant's office, before I could speak, Capt. Ambrose said, "That's it!"

"That's what?"

"Your it."

"Okay, I'm what?"

"You're my answer to a problem, I need a model for this afternoon."

"To model what, sir?"

"Yourself, as a Special Forces soldier." He went on to explain, "You know. Iron Mike."

"Of course." Iron Mike is the nickname for a large statue at the entrance to Fort Bragg.

"The photographer will be here at 1300 hours. Check out an AR15 and a .45 and come back with a full rucksack and pistol belt."

"Are they replacing Iron Mike?"

"No, I'm sure that's not going to happen. But the photos will be sent to an artist who will then create a statue. What happens after that, who knows?"

The shoot was over in less than an hour. I returned the weapons and my mind returned to being a lifer. What an honor to be selected as a Special Forces soldier!

Don't get a big head. You were just the right guy in the right place at the right time. Right place and time? Should that be Ozone Park in March 1965, with my new family?

The pros and cons bounced back and forth in my head like a tennis match. The serve! Showering with six guys at a time while a few others pass toilet paper back and forth. The return! A white porcelain tub with a shower curtain and bathmat, warm and soft. The volley continues! Short-haired guys sitting around in their boxers or the vision of Carol in that white peignoir set?

The match continued each day until the eyelids came down like the final curtain on an opera, only there was no applause. Daylight awakens the senses, a quick splash of water on my face, khaki shorts, a white T-shirt, and boots. Five miles later, the daily dozen, designed to build the entire body. Not sure I want to do this for 15 more years.

While on the other side of the net, the opposing player's visions were more vivid each day. The traditional house with a white picket fence and the 2.4 children. Fooling myself, pretending to use logic to make an intelligent choice, I listed the pros and cons.

Happy family man or trained killer.

Discharged and broke or re-up with bonus money.

Full-time wife or lonely nights.

Nice clean sheets or nights in the woods.

Good wholesome food or Army chow.

The deciding factor became our wedding vows; love, honor obey. Okay, not so much the obey part. Those vows were made before God and to Carol. So, I guess that means God is watching out for her. Who better to have in your corner than God almighty? It became clear, at least at that moment. God had the home-court advantage. Call it a small voice in my head, the power of prayer, or the exercise of intelligence. I had made up my mind.

"Hello Carol, it's me. I'm coming home this weekend. We need to talk."

13. Home Sweet Home

"Hi, honey, it's me. I'm on my way home, just outside of DC. Hope to be home by midnight, no later than one. Wait up for me, okay? Gotta go, love you."

Trips home were hectic and they only happened if there were four or five guys to share the cost of gas. If so, then the owner of the car would ride free. Switching drivers every few hours when we stopped for gas was like a NASCAR pit stop. Car serviced, we would pull around to pick up the last one out of the restroom and get back on the track. They were short weekends and every minute counted. Often the trip back was a brief exchange of our activities during our visits and soon the passengers would doze off, resting until their turn at the wheel.

This particular weekend, I shared my decision to not re-up. I told them my wife was overjoyed and her parents, I thought, were grateful that at last, we would be moving out of their house. Of course, they never came right out and said that. I was very truthful with my car mates, sharing my apprehension about not having a job and little savings. Leaving a "sure thing" was a leap of faith and I found I had none.

***

My last few months continued without incident. The occasional Sunday dinner with Alma and Don continued with Alma making it clear she would miss her boy toy.

Capt. Ambrose called me into his office one morning as my separation date approached. "I have something for you," handing me a brown envelope. "Here are the photos they took of you."

I started to ask questions, but he had no information except that an artist was working on a statue.

My separation in March 1965, involved a few steps: medical, dental, supply, and weapons clearance. I packed what was left into my duffel bag, having taken or shipped home most of my possessions. The last step was to pick up my separation orders, discharge papers (DD 214), travel voucher, and final payout. I had prepared for this day. My uniform was clean and pressed, my brass and boots spit-shined. Wow! No more guard mount, no more night jumps, no more daily five-mile runs, no more close-in combat training, or ration testing. Who are you kidding? You loved it and you know it.

I took a deep breath and stood before the full-length mirror as I donned the green beret for the last time. The red flash over the left eye, the rest draped softly to the right. A momentary cringe went through my whole body as I considered, once more, whether I was doing the right thing. Oh well, it's too late now. My last look. I'm proud of you, you earned it. You've done things some men only dream of doing.

***

My new civilian life was not as I had imagined. Because we were living in someone else's home, our quarters were cramped, privacy non-existent, and there was a general feeling that I was trespassing.

Our only private space was our small bedroom. With a full bed against the wall and the crib across the bottom, we were left with only a thin sliver of "toe stumping" space between the bed and the dresser. Carol slept on the outside, in case the baby needed attending during the night, which he often did. It brought back images of my childhood when I shared tight sleeping quarters with all my siblings. Needless to say, this did nothing for our love life.

The manners I was taught as a child made me hesitant to open their refrigerator. After all, it was their appliance and their food. That may have been juvenile, but certain things from childhood tend to stay with you. The whole thing drove me to look harder for a job if just to get me out of the house.

First stop, the New York Times want ads. The first ad did not supply much information aside from the fact that the position involved sales. The man who answered the phone also did not have a whole lot to say about the job. When I arrived at the address in Brooklyn where I was to fill out an application, I found that it was a luncheonette.

He explained, "This is where we meet every morning before we go out on sales calls." Both the application and interview were brief. Having completed both, I became a Fuller Brush man, going door-to-door peddling soap, brushes, and household items. I was less than thrilled about this but agreed to go out with a salesman to see what the job was all about.

I stood quietly beside him as we went door to door and he did his spiel. Which he did not do very well, in my opinion. The first afternoon that I was allowed to go out on my own, I went into an apartment building and began knocking on doors. After nothing but rejection from occupants who were simply not interested, I began to wonder if I had the wrong sales pitch. When the first door was slammed in my face, that was the end for me. I would never do that to anybody, and I wouldn't accept it being done to me. The job was definitely not for me.

The second ad sounded more promising; Monday through Friday truck driver. Well, there was something I knew I could do, and I would have weekends off. That would allow me to find a second job, maybe get a few bucks put away so that we could get out of her parents' house. I had to take a bus and train, then walk five blocks to the Elite Linen Company in Harlem to fill out an application. That walk was okay in daylight, but the job started at five in the morning. Walking the streets by myself at that hour did not sit too well. Although I was a retired badass, I was not a dumbass. Parading through a low-income, high-crime neighbor-hood in the dark was just asking for trouble.

My first interview was with a young man dressed in work clothes, definitely a blue-collar guy. That seemed to go well, and he then sent me off to be interviewed by the president of the company. As I sat in his office, I took in my surroundings and soon realized that this guy was an ex-marine. I should not say ex-marine, there are no ex-marines. Once a marine always a marine. It did not take long for him to get around to my military career. When I shared that I was a Special Forces vet, he hired me at once. I was set up with a Long Island route and introduced to a guy who would show me the ropes.

Mr. Hudson, a 6-foot-tall black man, was almost as wide as he was tall. When we were introduced, he looked at me with kind of a smile. I could not tell what he was thinking. When I told him I would have to travel through the subway and walk five blocks from the station to get to work, he laughed.

"Is that funny?" I asked.

"No." He pulled out a parka. It was big, blue, and heavy with "Elite Linen" embroidered across the back in white letters. "Nobody in the neighborhood will give you any trouble if they know you work for us. When you start?"

I said, "Tomorrow morning."

"Okay, I'll see you at 6 a.m. We'll be going out to Long Island. We have a hospital and a couple of restaurants and country clubs on the route."

At 4:45 in the morning, I successfully exited the house without waking anyone. The subway ride wasn't bad, but the walk from the station still had me on edge. It was kind of quiet on the street, but I kept my eyes open. When I got to the laundry, it was like a scene out of Porgy and Bess. There were many black men and women loading and sorting laundry in the street. It reminded me of black farm hands loading bales of cotton. I connected with Hudson, who gave me a few pointers on how to use the hand trucks, how to get the hampers stacked inside each other, and then how to get them on the lift gate. He certainly made it look effort-less.

When I tried, he stopped me. "You can't muscle it. Just use your head. Do it this way, use leverage. Tip the hampers, slide the hand truck in with your foot, lean it back. It's all about leverage. "Otherwise, you'll be exhausted by 4 o'clock and won't be able to stand up."

I looked him in the eye and said, "Thank you."

By 3:30 that afternoon, I was close to exhaustion. There was a lot to learn, not only the route and the locations but also how to get around. Each stop had a different system for delivery. After a week and a half, I was ready to go on my own. My last day with Hudson was a Friday, and our last stop that afternoon was Deep Dale Hospital in Queens.

We backed the truck down the ramp and opened the double doors. Hudson said, "We're running late. Let's not waste any time. Go to the first double doors on the right. All the soiled linen will be there waiting for you. Hurry up!"

With military precision, I did exactly as he said. I rushed down the ramp, threw open the double doors, and found myself standing in the middle of the morgue, witnessing a full-blown autopsy, I was just in time to see the doctor, organs in her hand, set them in a scale that looked misplaced from the produce section of the A&P. I was so surprised! She just said, "Can I help you?"

"No, no. I'm looking for soiled linen."

She realized I was the victim of a practical joke and said, "Down the hall." When I got back to the truck, Hudson was standing there laughing uncontrollably.

***

The Big Bow Wow, so named for its large hot dogs, was my first choice for a weekend job. Bullseye! It was a drive-up restaurant conceived by an Italian butcher and a Jewish businessman. Initially, it was simply a large, brick barbecue grill with roll-down doors; set back off a busy beach road. Cars would drive within feet of the counter to order hamburgers and hot dogs.

The place was a big hit, not only on summer beach days but year-round, day and night. Little by little the owners added outdoor tables, longer counters, and more menu items. By 1965 the employees were, for the most part, teenage boys in white pants and shirts and Norman Rockwellesque collapsible paper hats. I had initially hesitated at the sight of the paper hats, a far cry from a green beret. Do you want your own apartment or not? Yeah, yeah, swallow your pride.

The restaurant's expansion was extensive, seating no less than eighty at small Formica and chrome tables. There were several different stations: Deli, grill, corn on the cob, clam bar, drinks, and pizza. The length of the counter was about forty feet. Sunday afternoon during the summer, it was always jammed with people returning home from the beach.

I was trained on the grill and caught on quickly. The orders for steaks, burgers, and bow-wows were called in by the counter boys, in that sequence. Steaks were called my name, burgers, and bows by amount. So, an order for 2 steaks, 3 burgers, and 2 bow-wows would be called in as "2 steaks and a 3-2. The trick was to keep track of each order and shoot them back as fast as you could. Not an easy feat when most times six counter boys were shouting the orders. What made things even more difficult was the intense heat around the grill, well over 100 degrees. All this for the minimum wage of eighty cents an hour. I soon proved myself to be a punctual, reliable, and flexible employee. In addition to working the grill, I could open clams and fry fish and often worked the deli with Richard, who later dated my niece, Marilyn.

This seven-day rat race continued through the first summer following my discharge. Most days were worse than the PT at Fort Bragg. At least after five miles, you stopped and most weekends you were off. But every time I thought of quitting, the vision of my apartment flashed in my mind, sitting on the couch, cuddling with Carol and the baby. The idea of going to the fridge for a beer anytime I wanted, brought a smile and a burst of renewed energy.

***

Grace's husband, Bob, had been working for New York Telephone since his discharge from the Air Force Everyone knew the phone company didn't pay very well but it was a secure job. Bob had a friend in Personnel and asked if I was interested in applying. I was tested in the morning, interviewed in the afternoon, and slated to start in two weeks. That was the end of the truck driving job! I would be working in Brooklyn, at the same office as Bob, as a trunk assignor for $78 per week. A trunk assignor, in those days, would assign telephone cables. Each cable had hundreds of pairs of wires used for telephone transmissions. All the cables and wires were numbered and were designated for the splices to connect one cable to the other. These completed wires and cables formed a network that ran for hundreds of miles beneath the city streets.

I enjoyed the air-conditioned office, an hour for lunch, and a white shirt and tie. This also allowed me to work several nights a week at the Bow Wow. Within a month or two an apartment became available just across the street from my in-laws. Carol thought that was perfect and did not want to look any further. After some consideration, I decided that there were definite benefits; a built-in babysitter in her mother and a handyman, when needed, in Charlie. I admit that sometimes he made me feel useless and that often I let him.

***

My mother was admitted to Jamaica Hospital, the afternoon of February 10, 1967. She had been coughing up blood for some time, a condition that had been left unaddressed up to that point. A brutal snowstorm was brewing when I visited with her in the afternoon. The bleeding had been stopped and she was sitting on the edge of the bed, her legs dangling. I decided to go home and get off the roads, keeping a visual on the rapidly mounting snowdrifts. I had no sooner gotten into bed when the phone rang. Mom was not expected to make it through the night. All public transportation was shut down and the roads had not been plowed. My only choice was to dress as warmly as possible and walk. I arrived at her bedside as a nurse was removing a flexible gastro tube from her lifeless body. The cause of death was esophageal hemorrhage.

***

The following year, my brother Paul called me. "There's a job available at the St. Regis Hotel." He explained that his brother-in-law's brother-in-law worked there, and they needed a receiving clerk. The job paid $110 a week and included meals. The prerequisites were to keep your mouth shut and do as you're told.

"Can you live with that?"

"Are you kidding? I spent six years in the Army. I'm perfectly trained for that job."

So, after one year and 17 days, my secure job at New York Tel was ended. Who could blame me? A $32 a week raise!

The St. Regis was under new ownership. New owners, new rules. The steward who placed the orders could not be the person who received the deliveries. This was their attempt to eliminate an opportunity for someone to pad their pockets. Hence, my new job was to receive all food and groceries and check them against the hotel's guidelines and specifications. For instance, the rib eye roast had to have a 12-inch bone, the eye had to measure three inches by five inches and be a total weight of 38 pounds. Each piece of meat, whatever the cut, had to be tagged with a card listing the weight, description, and date received. The invoice for each was to be recorded, in duplicate, with dollar amounts totaled and extended at the end of the day. All deliveries had to be categorized as fish, dairy, meat, or dry goods. My desk was at the entrance to the storeroom. It was encased by glass windowpanes, giving me a view of the refrigerators, the scales, the butcher shop, and the fishmonger's workstation. Behind me, in the storeroom, were the dry goods.

Tony, the brother-in-law's brother-in-law, formerly had my job and had also been the Chief Steward. So, he had been ordering and receiving, the new corporation's no-no. He had now been moved into the food and beverage control office across the hall. He was about 5'8", 250 pounds with black hair pushed straight back, and his 5 o'clock shadow showed up at 9:30 every morning.

He took me on a tour through the kitchen. We went down the hall, and up a few steps, and into the bakery, where the bread and rolls were baked fresh every morning. The kitchen had separate stations for everything, sauté grill, soups, sauces, etc. I was shown the pantry where they made coffee, toast, and various breakfast items. At the end of the kitchen were the pastry shop and another bakery.

Tony greeted the three men there by name, turned to me, and said, "These men are absolute artists. You'll get to see some of their work later."

I asked, "How many guys work here?"

"There are one hundred. They work under the chef's supervision and are not all here at the same time." I just shook my head in amazement. On the way back, we stopped at the chef's office.

"Bonjour, bonjour." Chef Joseph seemed to be all business. He shared a few words with his secretary as Tony and I stood by waiting. I felt like I ranked with the lowest pot washer in the house.

Tony whispered, "He is the supreme ruler in this place, whatever he says, just do it. Capeesh?"

He then introduced me to Juan and Julio who were our storeroom guys. When they were not working there, they would be doing prep work for the kitchen. "Julio will get you coffee if you want and bring your lunch right to your desk on a room service cart. Just tell him what you want, and he'll get it for you."

About two days into my week of training, Tony handed me an invoice from Deep-Sea Seafood Company. "At the end of the day, add this to the log like you always do."

I must have had an inquisitive look on my face. He explained. "All fish comes in fresh from the market and is consumed on the day it is purchased. By morning, when the invoices are taken to accounts payable, there is no way to check the inventory."

After that, every day, five days a week, I added an invoice. At the end of the week, there would be over $1000 to split three ways among Tony, me, and the fish dealer. About three weeks later, he motioned me to the back of the storeroom and handed me an envelope. "Put this away, it will keep coming once a month. Keep your mouth shut. Capeesh?" Capeesh, I did!

I continued to advance in my new career. The chef became more friendly, and Tony was always nearby to answer any questions. Little by little, I was becoming more familiar with French terminology. I was getting comfortable with moving around the kitchen, mostly just to see what was going on. I quickly fell in love with the culinary arts. It wasn't just about cooking. What they did with food was a work of art.

About six months after I started, the executives decided the payroll needed to be trimmed. The bright guys on the fourth floor now wanted to know if I could do both jobs; ordering and receiving. This was the company no-no that led to my being hired in the first place.

"Well, yes, I know I could do it, but it would probably mean extending my workday." Are you ready for this? "I would have to be compensated in some way." They offered me an extra $20 a week, with the usual caveat about reviewing the arrangement in a couple of months. I graciously agreed. Frankly, I would have worked for less money as long as they kept ordering fish. As time went on, I was able to get cuts of meat like filets, ribs, and loins dropped off at a local butcher shop where I picked them up after work, all cut and wrapped in freezer paper. Our freezer, and that of my in-laws, was always full of the best meats.

***

One of the local watering holes on Liberty Avenue had a kitchen in the back room that was not being used. I spoke to the owner who said a few people had tried to make a go of it but had failed. He would love to have somebody open it on Friday and Saturday evenings to keep the crowd drinking longer. He gave me the go-ahead to put out a limited menu of burgers, sandwiches, and shrimp cocktails. Two weeks later I had a thriving small business going. Everyone was happy. I was working out of a cigar box for change and a cup for tips. Both were one hundred percent take-home pay.

One Saturday morning, I decided I needed some groceries. I went into the hotel and loaded up an empty egg crate that held about thirty dozen eggs. I filled it with groceries, meats, and things that I needed for the bar. I topped off the box with two layers of eggs, about 5 dozen or so, as camouflage, so no one could see what was underneath. I went out of the service entrance, using a pass that I had made out myself. By this time, everybody knew me, and I moved about without being questioned. That day, I walked outside, passed the main entrance to the hotel, and who steps out of the front door but the resident manager and the house detective.

"Good morning Mr. Banks. How are you?"

"Fine, Larry, where are you going with the eggs?"

"Land O' Lakes delivery came in late yesterday, so I borrowed some from the Gotham Hotel to hold us over. I'm returning them."

"Okay, have a good day."

I watched them as they stepped back into the building. I ducked between two cars and loaded the haul into my trunk. A close call!

I continued to use the hotel as the supply source for my kitchen. Now that I was "ordering and receiving" I could order in excess, mark it to be returned (having already worked a deal with the driver), and arrange to pick it up at another location. I did not overdo it, just enough to keep my business going. I suppose I was a typical thief. No matter how much you get you always want a little bit more.

My undeclared income put us in a position to splurge a bit. I was tired of driving the ten-year-old turquoise Chevy Bel Air that Charlie had given us and decided to buy a new '67 Chevy Impala. We had the apartment, all new furniture, and we were eating out more often than we should have, always with Beefeater martinis, fine wine, and cordials.

While I had expanded my vocabulary by picking up a few new cooking terms from "The Larousse Gastronomic" there were a few terms that had long been a part of my vocabulary: infidelity, incarceration, and pregnancy.

14. Ethics and False Piety

It was New Year's Eve, and my in-laws were hosting a small house party, just a few neighbors, family, and Dot's childhood friend, also named Dorothy, whom we called Aunt Dottie. When the countdown started 8-7-6 …, everyone gravitated to their partners, 3-2-1 "Happy New Year!" New Year's kisses and hugs were passed around in a friendly way. Stephanie Cox slipped me the tongue. What the hell was that? I was stunned. I tried to rationalize. Maybe she was missing Joe, who was still incarcerated, or she had simply had too much to drink. Certainly, she would not be making a pass in front of my wife and in-laws.

When the festivities slowly came to an end, Aunt Dottie needed a ride back to Brooklyn. Charlie was the intended designated driver, but his sobriety was in question. I offered, but it was pointed out that although I was sober, I had had a long day. Stephanie quickly offered to ride along to keep me alert. The ride to Aunt Dottie's was full of conversation about children and the two Dotties as teenagers. The passenger now delivered; Stephanie slid closer to me.

I asked, "What was that back at the house?"

"Didn't you like it?"

A mixture of awkwardness and excitement filled me as she stretched over to kiss me.

"Hey, I'm trying to drive."

"So, pull over."

And I did. I put the car in park and shifted my position, squaring my shoulders to have a conversation. She reached out and pulled my face closer. Conversation was the last thing on her mind. It became obvious to both of us that we were after the same thing. But not there and not then. We agreed to meet in the city where Stephanie's office was not too far from the hotel.

In the weeks that followed, we simply met after work, had a drink, and talked. The conversations centered around our individual sex lives and how she missed Joe. Sometimes I thought the conversations were foreplay, but our physical relationship never progressed beyond the New Year's Eve episode. The few times we traveled home together on the subway; we would split up for the walk home from the elevated station. It was a strange feeling, having a clandestine relationship with a neighbor and friend. We finally agreed that it was unfair to both Carol and Joe, in addition to being unhealthy. Our common sense prevailed and we agreed to stop meeting and to never speak of it again.

On what was to be our last "rush hour rendezvous," Stephanie casually mentioned that someone else had the hots for me. Flattered, I asked who. Flo, the third Lee sister.

"But isn't she married?" I quickly realized what a stupid question that was.

"She and Tony are separated, getting divorced," she said as she handed me Flo's number. I was not surprised. I recalled a night at Marlow's when he was sitting at the bar and Flo's mother came in and started screaming at him. According to her, Flo was pregnant by him, and she was loudly demanding he do the "right thing." He ignored her as long as he could, then hit her so hard she went backward over the skee ball machine.

I stuck the phone number in my pocket. On the walk home, I wondered if Steph was trying to assure our separation would last by getting me into another affair. I played with the idea of calling Flo and a few days later decided to stop by for the proverbial cup of coffee and attempt to get to the truth. We had an interesting conversation. It seemed that Stephanie had told Flo that I had the hots for her. She was playing both ends against the middle. Here I was, a guy in good health and stamina, who thought with his organ and not with his brain, with two women whose sexual appetites had been deprived by separation from their spouses. No surprise where this was going.

Flo and I arranged to see each other at her apartment, at all hours of the night, over several weeks. We both knew it would go nowhere. On the night we agreed to stop seeing each other, she took me by the hand and led me into the kitchen. We sat down in the glow of the open refrigerator. "Larry, if you weren't married, I wouldn't want you to go. You have taught me the difference between having sex and making love. With Tony, it was just sex and he used me like an animal. You made me feel good about myself."

I cupped her face in my hands, "That's the way it's supposed to be and I'm happy for you." I gently kissed her good night and never saw her again.

***

It was Monday morning at about 10 when the phone rang. It was Mr. Herman, the food and beverage director.

"Larry I just wanted to make sure you were in. I'm coming down. I want to talk to you."

"Very good, I'll be here." Oh crap, he never comes down here. There must be a problem. I stepped across the hall to see Tony.

"Tony! Herman's coming down here. I don't know what he wants."

"Don't worry. He doesn't know anything. Just keep your mouth shut."

Herman was a stocky man, about 60 years old, with just a little bit of gray hair on each side at his temples. His protruding stomach precluded him from buttoning his jacket.

"Good morning, Mr. Herman. What can I do for you?"

"No, Larry it's what I can do for you. You have been doing a good job for several months with the purchasing and receiving. I would like to round out your experience by moving you over to the wine cellar."

"I... I... don't know very much about wine."

Expounding in a boastful way, "It's the third-largest wine cellar in the city. It will be a great opportunity to learn about wine and controlling inventory. We have faith in your abilities. You will start next Monday. Until then, go over and look around. Become familiar with the area."

He was gone as quickly as he had appeared. All the blood drained from my head as I envisioned a red tide and all my fish dying in a sea of money. After the initial shock, I theorized that beverages must work the same way as other inventory. This hotel's room service, bar, and banquet rooms must dispense enough booze to float a battleship! I'll just have to feel my way around.

The wine cellar was gigantic, entered through a large door off one of the underground hallways. The floor was tiled in black and white hexagon marble, and thirty feet into the enormous room was my new desk. The walls were lined with shelves supporting thousands of bottles of liquor and wine. Rooms were set aside to separate wines by country. There were chateau wines, regional wines, some with names I couldn't even begin to pronounce. The regional wine room had a large round table and a slop sink which had originally been used for wine tastings.

I soon learned to sip, swish, and aerate, before swallowing. Rarely did I spit it out. Two large walk-in refrigerators, one loaded with champagne, the other for the banquet department, secured all the open bottles of liquor. Inside that walk-in was a priceless learning experience.

Now I could taste wine with my lunch and after, have a cordial or two. Just for educational purposes, of course. Every day was like a wine tasting. I kept telling myself this was part of my food and beverage education. Amazing! A few months before, I hadn't known the difference between endive and chicory and now I didn't know the difference between chardonnay and burgundy.

Another interesting point, in traditional French cuisine it is customary to supply wine or beer to the kitchen staff. In our case, each man received two bottles of beer per day to have with his meals. It was my job to keep a supply of less-expensive beer to the tune of 100 cases a month.

One day Carol called, "Someone wants to deliver five cases of Heineken beer. What should I do?"

"Accept it. It must be a gratuity from one of the dealers. I wasn't expecting it, but it's okay."

It was also my job to order wine, beer, and liquor for upcoming events, parties, wedding banquets, etc. that had specified a particular brand or vintage. The state liquor authority had control over which companies had distributorship for which labels. You could only order "brand A" from "company X." No one else could sell that brand. I had no choice but to work within those parameters.

Mr. Herman waddled into the wine cellar one Monday. "Have you ordered the champagne for the Rothschild party this week?"

"Yes, sir. Fifty cases of the Dom Perignon. It came in Friday and it's already on ice."

"Who did you order it from?"

"ABC company"

"Oh, no. You should have ordered it from XYZ. Call ABC and send it back. Then reorder from XYZ."

"But I've already thrown the boxes out."

"Re-order. When they come in, send them back to ABC in XYZ's boxes."

Here is where I get stupid, very stupid. I was well on my way to setting up my own "relationship" with ABC and this was going to put a serious wrench in the works. I was scrambling for something to say that might change Herman's course, when I blurted out, "No, that's immoral, I mean it's not right to cancel that big an order."

Now he is looking at me as though I have lost my mind, and quietly, but firmly says, "I have an arrangement with XYZ."

Displaying my false moral integrity, "How was I supposed to know that? I can't be a party to such things. I would rather leave my keys on the desk and walk out."

"Okay, then leave them."

Suddenly, that misstep assured me there would be no more envelopes in my future.

When I talked to Tony, he said "You should never have put his back to the wall. Just do as you're told."

***

Taking pity on me, Tony put me in touch with another of his connections. He sent me over to Madison Square Garden, which was still under construction, but the 48-lane bowling alley had a restaurant and bar that needed a manager. After a rather brief interview, the job was mine.

The Garden's opening was coming up and concession stands were being stocked. Hundreds of hawkers would be selling hundreds of thousands of dollars in merchandise during events. I started thinking, in an operation that big, they would never miss a few bucks each night from the bowling alley snack bar. Wrong! When confronted, I denied, denied, denied... but they did not buy it. Game over. Suddenly, I'm in a world of doodoo. No job, no side businesses, and a pregnant wife.

Once again, I am rescued. It's midnight when the phone rings. It was Claudia's husband, Joe. "Hey Larry, you want to work tonight? They're short in the comics section."

"Sure, what do I have to do."

"Come to the Brooklyn plant. Go to the third floor, turn left out of the elevator, and walk to the back of the press room. Ask for Duffy and wear old clothes."

"Okay, thanks, Joe."

While driving down Atlantic Avenue, I couldn't help but think about how great my brothers-in-law had been to me. Tommy, Joan's husband, had given me my first car. Marilyn's husband, Lou, was a big hunk of a man, whose bear hug could cuddle or crush you. But he never uttered a foul word. He introduced me to stock car racing at Dexter Park, where we would go every Thursday night. I loved to sit down next to the track at the finish line, hear the screaming engines, smell the burning rubber as they roared, three abreast, into the first turn; always knowing something had to give and waiting for the collision. Then, of course, there was Bob, Grace's husband, who got me into the phone company and helped many times in many ways. I wondered how much influence my sisters had over their husbands on my behalf. I am and will remain, ever thankful for the part they played in my growth, experience, and in the case of Joe, a 37-year career in newspaper printing.

One hour later, I was looking for a safe, well-lit parking spot. Before entering the elevator, I recognized the sound of production spiraling down the shaft to street level. The steel freight car's wire gates closed before the heavy outer doors slammed together. First stop, the reel room on the second floor, affording me a momentary glance as three men exited. Tremendous rolls of paper hummed as they spun, unwinding like giant rolls of toilet paper, pulled by a playful child. On the third floor, I stepped onto the steel diamond-plate flooring, where the humming became a deafening roar. Peering through the ink mist, I see the paper from the floor beneath take a magical journey of twists and turns, seemingly exceeding the speed limit. Two rolls feeding to the left, three others whizzing to the right, all converging in the space that would be the fourth floor. Mysteriously sandwiching one over the other, folding and descending into a machine with massive drums that banged with each rotation, severing the collected sheets. The volume, speed, and flickering lights of the presses caused instant tension and the awareness of danger. Avoiding a mop bucket full of kerosene, I took three steps and craned my neck. More right angles and the finished papers were ascending again, across the room, down the enclosed shaft, and out of sight.

"Mr. Duffy, I'm Larry Phillips. Joe Peers told me to ask for you."

"Okay, Larry. Give me your Social Security card and fill out this paper. You can do it in the locker room, over there. Stay with the guys, have a beer. I'll come and get you when I need you."

Have a beer? Yeah, right. I entered a filthy, ink mist painted room with rows of full-length lockers separated by benches. The benches were dark with years of ink, either transferred or rubbed into them from the work clothes of the men who rested on them. To my surprise, four guys in blue coveralls huddled around a five-gallon plastic bucket full of beer on ice. My Social Security deduction paper was a dead giveaway. "First day?" Said one of the four. "You want a beer?"

Stammering "I... I... I have to go to work. Mr. Duffy is going to come for me when he needs me."

"So, have a beer until he comes." Another of the four, an older man explained. "There's nothing you can do. It's a "make ready." You got lucky tonight."

"I don't understand."

"Make ready is making the press ready for the next run of comics. They are printed weeks in advance. Without any experience, you would only be in the way. So, have a beer."

So far everyone I had met had encouraged me to have a beer.

"Okay, I'll have one, only one. Who do I pay?"

"Nobody. It's all paid for."

Two beers later, Mr. Duffy came into the locker room. "Give me the paper so you can get paid and then go home."

"But I didn't do anything."

"Yeah, I know. We're all finished for the night. Go home."

"Will I get paid?"

"Yes, now go home. If I need you again, I've got your number."

"Yes, please call me. I owe you one."

"Okay kid, I like that."

The next night the phone rang. Without hesitation, "Yes sir I'll be right in."

"Hi, Phillips, tonight you can get your hands dirty."

"Just tell me what to do."

Outfitted with long heavy-duty gloves, I spent two-and-a-half hours washing blocks and end seals. Another part of the press had huge clumps of dried ink. I scoured the parts in a plastic bucket like the one that had chilled the beer the night before. The solvent used was strong, strong enough to get you high if you sniffed just a little. I was instructed to put large sheets of cardboard on the floor and to avoid breathing the fumes.

"Hey, Phillips, nice job. Just pick up the rags and mop up any puddles or grease. Then go home."

"Mr. Duffy, I haven't been here three hours yet."

"Our regular guys will take care of the rest. Have a good night."

"Good night, thank you." That was the easiest $52 bucks I had ever made.

The next day Joe called me. "How did you do?"

"I did fine. I mean, I did nothing. What a job, paid to drink beer."

"If you want to work you have to show up at the shape room every night at 7:30. It's in Manhattan on 42nd Street and Second Avenue, third-floor. All the jobs are doled out then. Even the late floors and the Brooklyn jobs. Some start as late as 11:30." Listen up, he went on, "If you go, there is no legal parking on the street until 7 p.m. If you park before then, the meter maids will ticket your car.

And with that, my career began!

I worked many late floors, sweeping and bailing up wastepaper. It was impossible to stay clean. The ink mist was in the air circulating throughout the entire room. By morning light, the sun's rays pierced the windows on the south wall, highlighting the fine mist which fell like a light dusting of snow. The "black snow" settled in my ears and nostrils, and I thought I would never have clean hands again. Thirteen months later, I had worked the 104 required number of days in a six-month period which entitled me to a union card. I paid the initiation fee and dues, and my name went to the top of the shape list.

Joe called again, "If you want a steady job, some bids are opening on the midnight roto. That's short for rotogravure, the magazine section of the Sunday paper. It's a different type of printing and it's a hand fly. They'll teach you how to "fly n' carry."

The fly was the name for the conveyor that carried the papers to the mail room and the loading platform. In the roto, the papers were stacked on skids and held to be inserted into the paper later. That meant no more late floors, no more driving into Manhattan, and normal parking.

Joe told me how to put in my bid and then I waited. The results would be posted at the designated date and time. I was convinced I could learn anything if given a chance. Three weeks later, the bids were posted, and my name was on the list for the midnight roto. I was officially a roto dodo, an affectionate term for the guys in the roto.

***

"Here's the deal" as I was set upon in the locker room by the team. There are four boys to a press, two early and two late. When you're early, you leave at 3:30 am. Late, you stay until seven in the morning. You cannot go home if you can't fly and carry. When you're in, you work half hours with your partner, a half-hour in then half-hour break. If you get behind, drop the papers. You will have to pick them up, count, and bundle them on your own time.

I then got a short lesson from Jimmy The press started up slowly and Jimmy explained his movements.

"Every fifty papers has a kick sheet." One paper kicked out at an angle. "Watch my hands. I push the papers back up the conveyor, use my thumb in place of the kick sheet, and collect the fifty papers in my two hands. I break them against my stomach, jog them on the top of the steel table, swivel to the left, and place them on this skid. Eleven bundles to a layer, with each layer turned opposite of the one beneath. Want to try?"

"I guess I have to."

"Okay, get a hamper." They were exactly like laundry hampers. "Put it next to the fly. If you can't keep up, just throw them in the hamper. Later, you'll get to pick them up. The pressman will not slow the press down. If he stops the press, you're both in trouble."

My first attempt went into the hamper. Jimmy shouted, "Push back, use your thumb to break, jog, stack. Push back, use the thumb, jog, stack. Push back, use the thumb, jog. You have to set it to music." The hamper was full in the first two minutes.

"Oh, shit, Jimmy. Get another hamper."

"Okay, get out."

I stepped aside. He was doing my work as I started sorting the papers in the hamper.

"Not as easy as it looks."

"Don't worry, you'll catch on. It will be as easy as walking."

He was right. In a few weeks, I was as good as any of the regulars. In time, I was showing off by doing push-ups between bundles.

That was the beginning of a ten-year stint as a roto dodo. The roto was a straight time job, with little overtime. But it allowed me to work other jobs. I had all day and most of the evening to rest before I went back to my three-and-a-half-hour shift. While that information was not exactly top-secret, I didn't go around advertising it either. I was still cherry-picking my hours at the Bow Wow. I would stay late at the roto and open the Bow Wow with Richie in the morning.

***

Carol and I took a ride out on Long Island and stumbled upon a model home in the town of Brentwood. I slowed as we passed, and we turned to each other with an inquisitive look. I made a U-turn. We were not shopping and had no idea what it would cost. The gravel and blue stone parking lot crunched under our feet as we made our way to the door. A pregnant couple with a three-year-old, we entered the high ranch, six steps up, where we were greeted by a gentleman.

"Hi, I'm Joe Maza, the builder."

"Hi, Joe. We were just passing by and thought we might take a look. If that's all right?"

"Sure, if you have any questions, just ask."

As the inspection commenced there were three bedrooms, a Jack and Jill bath, and "Look honey, wrought iron rails."

And as we descended to the family room, "Look, look, a pass-through into the two-car garage. Do you see this? Another bathroom down here. Holy cow, sliding glass doors to the backyard."

Carol whispered to me, "I'll bet it cost a fortune. Let's ask."

"Mr. Maza, how much?"

"$19,999."

"You mean $20,000."

"Well yeah."

"How much for the land?"

"That's included."

"What about clearing the land?"

"Included, $20,000 in the door. I've got a few lots you could look at."

"One more question, Joe. How much down?"

"About $4000."

"Can we go look at the lots now, while we're out here?"

"Sure, let's go to West End Avenue. It's a nice dead end and I have a few lots left."

Returning home, we shared with the family the excitement of seeing the model home and the prospect of a lot on a dead-end street. We also shared we were $2000 short of a down payment. Carol and I decided to try to save more.

The following Sunday, a personal phone call triggered panic in my mind while I was working the Bow Wow grill. It was over 100 degrees, and the crowd of scantily clad beachgoers was three deep at the counter.

Passing the spatula and thongs off to another, I grabbed the receiver. "What's the matter?"

"Nothing. My mother wants to ask you something."

"Yeah, mom, what's up? Is Charlie okay?"

She answered in her usual slow, detailed way "I know you're busy but…"

"But what, mom?"

"We took a ride today…"

"Yeah," now my patience was wearing thin.

"Carol took us to see the house... you know, and the lots on West End Avenue?"

"Yeah, mom"

"Would you mind if we bought the same house across the street?

"You're going to move, too?"

"Yes, we'll sell our house and move with you. Do you mind?"

"No. Do whatever you want. I couldn't stop you even if I wanted to." Hell, that made my answer sound like I didn't want them to sell. I rushed on "It's okay. Sure, it's okay. I got to go, bye."

I learned later, when I went to collect my family, that the phone call had been made from Joe Maza's office. They had made a

verbal commitment for both houses. Taken completely by surprise, I reminded them that we did not have the four grand. They
agreed to loan us whatever we needed, and we could pay it back
when we had it. While this took care of our money issue, there
were pros and cons. Would having my in-laws across the street
be a help or hindrance? It had been working so far and the idea of
having someone close by when I worked nights was appealing. It
seemed the positives outweighed the negatives.

This called for a celebration. We all had a drink and toasted
our new homes on Long Island. The next six months were nonstop work. We had borrowed $2000 from the in-laws and were
able to pay it back and still have the four grand we needed.

15. I Know About You and Steph

When Joe was scheduled to be released from prison, his in-laws did not want the junkie ex-con in their apartment. Knowing he would not be safe in Ozone Park where he had ripped off half the community, he and Stephanie moved out to a Long Island apartment complex. Hoping that getting Joe out of the drug environment in Queens would solve their issues, they started from scratch with their four-year-old, Debbie. Things were going well. Everyone was working and saving money and soon they could buy a small lot with hopes of building a house of their own.

Anxious to move into our new home, Carol and I made occasional trips to check the progress. One Sunday afternoon, we included Stephanie, Joe, and the kids. As we strolled down the grassy mall in the town of Watermill, with our families walking ahead of us, Joe blurted out, "I know about you and Steph." Stunned, I stammered, not knowing if he was testing me or if she had told him. Before I could reply, he strongly said "If it happens again, I will kill you. Now, we will never speak of this again."

"Okay but…"

"Not another word." And there never was.

***

I heard a crashing sound from the bathroom. Stephanie and Carol had taken the kids shopping, and Joe and I were alone in their apartment.

"Joe, are you okay?"

"Oh, shit" was his reply.

I opened the door and found he had lost his balance while trying to shoot up. He was either using again or had never stopped.

"Here, hold this," as he handed me the elastic band he had affixed as a tourniquet He had a small bottle cap, with a hairpin looped around it as a handle. "I need this. Help me before they get back."

Before I could utter words of discouragement, the hot juice was in the bulging vein.

I couldn't believe he had put me in such a position. What was he thinking to have that shit in the house? If he had overdosed, I would have been involved in his criminal activity. Days later we had a long talk and he promised me it had just been "a taste." He claimed he wasn't hooked because he got clean in jail. I thought if he stayed busy working, he wouldn't be tempted to get high. But I learned that working was an avenue to opportunity. An opportunity to make connections, money, and to find easy marks to rip off.

***

Stephanie went ahead with plans and permits for the new house. This was all on Steph. Joe was good with his hands but applying for and filling out the necessary paperwork had to be done by someone else. Joe's brother, Walter was an experienced construction worker and agreed to be the superintendent, if Joe could get the material and volunteer labor. I signed on with the rest of Cox's Army: Dennis, the butcher; Richard's delivery service; Billy, the produce worker; and Arthur, the realtor.

It was impressive to watch Walter direct six or seven guys. "You two cut 32 two-by-fours to 7'4" and you two set up the sawhorses to cut some plywood." And so it began. A few weeks later, it was ready for flooring and sheet rock, taping, and paint.

One evening, over a few cold beers Walter and I had a conversation about his side job. "I have a grocery store." That started me off with a bunch of questions about the location and suppliers. Finally, Walter admitted, "It's not really a store, it's a scam. I collect discount coupons. The ones they print in the newspapers. I cut them out and mail them to the clearing house. They, in turn, mail me a check for the amount plus a bonus of about five cents each."

"You mean like 25 cents off on a box of corn flakes? You have an imaginary grocery, like a kid with an imaginary friend?"

"Only they send checks to my imaginary store."

Walter was taken aback when I said, "I may be able to get you some coupons," explaining that I worked in the plant where those pages of coupons were inserted into the Sunday paper.

The News had good security systems in place to limit pilferage and keep workers, especially drivers, from starting their own paper route. But, no one paid much attention to the coupons bundled in hundreds that sat in the storage area, weeks in advance. On the midnight shift, there was no one around to question me when I took one or two bundles to my car on my way out.

Walter answered the door with scissors in hand. "Come in, come in."

The apartment was borderline hoarder's lair. Empty beer cans sat on every shelf and stacks of musty newspapers, in hastily tied bundles, were stored in what would be the living room. The nerve center for this high-tech operation included one folding table, a rickety-looking chair, and a Royal manual typewriter. A pile of papers, with coupons removed, were en route to the end of the production cycle.

"A hundred bucks a bundle," interrupts my inspection. "How many can you get?"

"How about two a week?"

"Deal."

Just like that, I was a silent partner in an imaginary grocery store. Six months into this enterprise, I stopped to make my weekly delivery. Walter wasn't home so I left the bundles at his door. The following week, I returned to do the same. The bundles were gone and so was Walter.

I questioned the building super who related "Two gentlemen came looking for him. I overheard them ask him "Where's your grocery store?"

When Walter admitted he didn't have a physical location, the two men identified themselves as FBI agents and arrested him for mail fraud. With that news, I swiftly exited down the hall and out the door, trying to look natural and hoping not to meet other agents. Each day I thought I could be next. Each night I avoided the storage area where the coupons were stored. Then I received word Walter had been sentenced to seven years.

***

One Saturday, just after midnight, the phone rang. "It's Joe. I'm in trouble. I fucked up."

"Tell me what you did." His hesitation told me it must be drugs. He had fallen off the wagon.

"I am near Marlowe's; I took some bad shit..."

"Sit still. I'll be there in ten minutes."

As I slipped into my pants, I told Carol I had to go help Joe. Sleepily she inquired "What's wrong? What happened?"

"He must've gone into the city for a drug connection." I stuck my bare feet into my sneakers. "He's in trouble. I'll find him." Driving up Lefferts Boulevard, I scoured the area for Joe. I had just made a U-turn and was headed back when I spotted what appeared to be a pile of rags against the building. My high beams revealed it was Joe. I quickly pulled my car to the curb.

"Joe, wake up. Joe, get up. Joe, Joe! What did you take? Joe, talk to me."

He was limp and heavy as I tried to get him up. Not knowing how to treat him I only knew what I had seen in the movies. Don't let him sleep, keep him walking.

"Walk, Joe, walk." With his arm draped over my shoulder, I involuntarily gave way to his leaning and staggering. Crying and sniffling as we walked, he said "I fucked up, man."

"Yes, you did but we'll get you through it." He reeked of vomit and urine.

"Joe, what did you take?"

"It was only a taste."

• *142* •

"What, Joe, what?"

Realizing it didn't matter, whatever he took I didn't have an antidote for it. Slowly he began to come around and tried to free himself from my grip. "Hold on. Where are we going? I need to sit."

"No way, Joe. Keep walking."

We were approaching Rockaway Boulevard and Lefferts, the hood of my youth. At every doorway, Joe wanted to sit and sleep. I wasn't sure if I was right, but I had to keep him moving. Now at 117th Street, just ten blocks from my apartment, with a sudden surge of energy, Joe pulled away, took a three-step run, and jumped spread eagle against a plate glass window. My heart was pounding as I watched this half-cooked noodle of a man fall to the concrete in a fetal position.

"I can't even fuckin' kill myself."

"No, Joe. God doesn't want you yet." We talked, we walked, we cried, we agreed he needed help. He told me of a hospital in Manhattan that had a rehab program. I learned later it was a methadone clinic, Joe knew it and was conning me. By now he needed another fix. He was most agreeable and told me what I wanted to hear. I was his ride and he knew I wanted to save him and his family. Junkies are deceitfully clever, with no allegiance to anything but their next fix. We arrived at Metropolitan Hospital's emergency room to learn that the drug rehab clinic was closed on Sunday. I was incredulous, "That's crazy! You can only get sick during the week" I knew sick wasn't the right word. "Can't you admit him to the hospital until tomorrow?"

The doctor was frank. "He's not sick. He is strung out and he needs a fix. If I give him what he wants, the line of junkies will be out to the street and around the corner." Joe became indignant and angry, or pretended to be, and stormed out of the ER.

"I'll take care of myself. Thanks, man. I'll be okay" As he walked away, I chased after him.

"Joe come home with me."

"No, man, I'll treat myself."

I knew what that meant. He would steal something or sell himself to get a fix on the streets of Harlem. I stood on the sidewalk, looking up at the giant mass of concrete and glass. Slowly I looked down and shook my head in resignation. I could not help Joe.

God, I hope you have a plan, was my prayer.

Making my way back to the car, I passed a building covered with graffiti. What a perfect depiction of Joe's life. Misshapen words spread over a coarse, impenetrable shell. Then I saw a dead bird in the gutter. OH NO, DEAR GOD, NO. Was this an omen of his plan for Joe?

***

Well, I have arrived at last! I admit, I may have begged, borrowed, and stole to get there, but suburbia has accepted me. Correction! Number one, I did not beg. Number two, although I had borrowed, I had also paid it all back. That must say something about my character. As for number three, at the least, I intended that "stole" remain in the past tense. And had suburbia accepted me, or had I simply imposed myself upon it?

Between being a Roto Dodo at night and a Bow Wower by day, lay a honey-do list that got longer and longer. We needed a fence, the lawn was seeded but with little or no effect, and the rough grading had left rocks and building material rising to the surface. Of course, a pool would be nice. Then there are the requisite toys, school clothes, bicycles; now that we lived in the country on a dead-end street, and on and on. The list was never-ending.

My day schedule at the Bow Wow allowed me just enough time to merge into rush-hour commuter traffic. After I found myself dozing off in bumper-to-bumper traffic, I began taking a 12-ounce cup of coffee with me for the drive home. Coffee worked, but soon I found one cup was not enough. I found myself biting my fingernails after the third cup, and I was still 30 minutes away. The commute often added an hour to the workday. Someone suggested I smoke so I would have something to do with my hands. No, I do not smoke. Don't want to and can't afford to. How about a cigar? Cigar, cigar echoed in my mind. You don't inhale and one would last the whole trip. One cigar is cheaper than a pack of cigarettes. Why not, after all, I've made it. I have a job, or should

I say a position, with the prestigious New York Daily News and a home on Long Island. I was convinced. I deserved a good cigar. Feeling good about myself was one thing, the image presented to onlookers another. I was still a smooth-faced, young-looking guy, who could shave every other day and still look clean cut. But with the cigar… maybe not.

I continued to work both jobs, taking the later half of the shift at the Roto and opening the Bow Wow in the morning. The house chores received attention, as time allowed. My family was growing, and we were spending more time together. Evenings in the family room around the TV, board games, and marathon tickling sessions brought me happiness and pride.

One night, after the kids were in bed and the late news was over, Carol suggested we go up.

"No, I just want to lay here for a few minutes."

With a puzzled look on her face, "Okay, but don't spend the night here."

I remember that night so clearly. I was savoring the room. Mostly the wood-paneled walls, extremely popular in the 60s, the Danish modern furniture, also in vogue, and the 12 x 12 rug that doubled as a wrestling mat. I was proud of myself. I had never known anyone, except in the movies, who had a paneled den with an adjoining bathroom. We had a kitchen and a dining room. I wondered if Carol shared my enthusiasm. She never said, "thank you" or "I appreciate all the work that you do." It seemed that our conversations centered around what material item or venture was next on the list. Was I just feeling sorry for myself?

We had decided that we needed to work on our relationship; material, spiritual, and sexual. Materially, we had everything we needed to get by but we did not have a dollar in the bank. What if we needed cash for repairs or anything unexpected? Her answer was, "We could borrow it from my mother." Not a good way to live. More than a few times we had resorted to the "National Bank of Across the Street." Each time it made me feel just a little inadequate. I brought home the money and Carol managed the household and the bill paying. She refused to open a checking account, saying that she preferred money orders. I tried to explain the convenience of having an account, but she chose to keep individual envelopes for each expense. She would cash my weekly checks and divvy up the money among the assigned envelopes. Every time I suggested anything else, it only led to a fight. After a while, I accepted it just to keep the peace.

On the spiritual front, Carol wanted to go back to church, citing that the boys should have some religious education. The very thought of Catholic religious education sent up a mental roadblock for me. I would not expose my children to that. After a search, the road led to the Lutheran church that sponsored a Cub Scout pack. Our first Sunday service was so different from the Catholic mass. The only celebrant was the pastor, and the liturgy was all in English, no Latin.

The pastor seemed a bit effeminate. I poked Carol and I raised my hand about three inches above my lap, stretched my fingers out, and rocked it left and right. After church, Carol asked what I thought.

"Well, let me see. There is no reverence, everyone talks, the kids all over the place, and Pastor Jones is as queer as a three-dollar bill." I suggested we continue the discussion at home where I was accused of being judgmental.

"Perhaps I am. But don't forget, I was a street-smart kid. I've been exposed to gay men and pedophiles."

"Oh yeah, just when was that?" I explained about the Hotel St. George and the barber from down Rockaway Boulevard who had a small apartment behind his shop. Of course, he was nice, and soon he was doing to me what I used to do to myself.

"There are things I don't know about the man I married?"

"Yes, some things are better left unsaid." That just brought more questions and did nothing to change her opinion that I was judgmental.

***

Now, it's 1969. Going into the fifth year of our sexual relationship, we had worked our way through "The Joy of Sex" which was larger than the Betty Crooker cookbook. There were others, of course, some pornographic, all to heighten foreplay and bring about climax for Carol. We had even consulted a professional counselor who suggested an open marriage. That was never going to happen! Well, it was an open marriage, but it was only open on my side. It was often frustrating. I felt as though I had to perform. What should have been love-making, ended with heated conversations, belligerent attitudes, and more peace talks than the United Nations. For years, I lived a life of "peace at any price."

Balancing semi-contentment and frustration left me open to even the slightest form of temptation. Stopping for a drink on the way home became a good idea. Pretty soon, one drink became two or three, and then stopping on the way to work seemed reasonable. After a while, you form a circuit, starting to meet new people. One of those new people was an entrant in an upcoming wet T-shirt contest. If size was a prerequisite, she was a front runner. This encounter proved to be regrettable. Moving in with the first-place winner was a very stupid thing to do.

I called Carol to explain my whereabouts and to tell her that I wanted a trial separation. She was only half surprised. I called every day to check on her and the kids. On the fourth day, I returned home. The repercussions at home proved you may forgive but you never forget. The psychological scars of my infidelity surfaced from time to time for the rest of our marriage.

I knew it was my fault. I did nothing to resist. Whether it was the overly friendly den mother or the 19-year-old who was barely legal, I just could not pass on any opportunity. I knew my reckless behavior, often with perfect strangers, was dangerous both medically, financially, and legally. The house I worked so hard for could all be lost with one bang of the judge's gavel.

I asked myself if I was a sexual addict and answered in the same breath. No! I do not need sex like a junkie needs a high. However, if it's available I'll take part. So, you could say I was a user, but not an addict. Did I need help? How the hell could I get help on my schedule and without exposing myself for what I was, addicted or not.

Life continued to sail by. The boys were both in school, and the parents were still smoking, drinking, and endlessly working on their relationship. Just an average suburban family, taking part in Cub Scouts, church services, and the PTA; until Carol became sick.

It began with unexplained vomiting. We tried to self-diagnose. It must be something you ate, a stomach virus, etc. When none of this panned out, we consulted a real professional. Dr. Chaudhry, who was also treating her for anxiety. He wrote a few prescriptions which did not do much. Despite our efforts to adjust her intake of food and drink, nothing seemed to work. On more than one occasion I found myself comforting her with a wet washcloth, sometimes retching right beside her.

After repeated office visits, the doctor suggested she come in while she was having the symptoms. I bit my tongue. I wanted to say, "Yeah, asshole, at 6 a.m. or 11 p.m." I truly had too much respect for the medical profession to say what I was thinking.

***

One day, while working at the Bow Wow, I received a call from Carol's sister, "Carol's in the hospital."

"What happened?" Carol had told her that she wanted to kill herself and Barbara called the doctor. He admitted her at once to South Oaks Psychiatric Hospital.

I raced to the hospital. Following the signs to the visitor's entrance, I encountered strict security. After many questions, I was finally escorted to her room. It was more of a cell. A steel frame bed, resembling an army cot, with a sagging mattress and nothing else. When I surveyed the room, I noticed there were quilted blankets on the walls like the kind moving men put over your furniture. Suddenly, it struck me that this was the proverbial "padded cell."

She just sat on the bed, in hospital scrubs, staring at the floor.

I went and sat at her side. "What happened? What did you do?"

She raised her head briefly, shrugged her shoulders, and continued to stare at the floor. Her eyes seemed glassy. I assumed she had been medicated or perhaps she was crying, or both. We sat together for several hours. My efforts to coax her to open up to me were fruitless. Her evening meal came, and I explained that I had to go home and take care of the boys. I promised to come back first thing in the morning. She gave me a half nod and then pushed away the untouched food tray.

As I exited the double doors, the locks clicked behind me. Pushing back the tears, I walked the long corridor to the exit. When the cold evening air hit my flushed face, I felt a spasm in my diaphragm, dryness in my throat, and tears started. I sat in the car, repeatedly pounding on the steering wheel, asking myself "What have I done? What have I done?"

16. *Neurological to Gastrointestinal*

The doctors decided that the suicidal thoughts were the result of the Prozac prescribed by Dr. Chaudhry. Once off the medication, she started feeling better but remained in therapy for another 27 days. If I ever had any negative thoughts about my in-laws living across the street, they turned 180 degrees during that period. I had never been so grateful.

The gastrointestinal problems continued, sometimes worse than others. While making plans for a Labor Day family barbecue, she had a severe attack. Dr. Chaudhry was not available, and my call was forwarded to Dr. Alpine who was covering for the weekend. He asked for some background and I explained the history of the phantom episodes. He. suggested doubling the dose of her prescribed meds. Approximately eight hours later, another round of dry heaves. When I called back, the doctor agreed to meet us at Good Samaritan Hospital emergency.

He was already there when we arrived and after a quick consultation, he ordered blood work. Taking me aside he explained, "I have ordered a test. But if she has what I think, she will be a very sick girl. It will be a few hours before the lab work comes back. They are making her comfortable. I'll be back later."

He returned in about two hours. "Larry, it came back positive. She has pancreatitis. I am admitting her and we'll do more tests tomorrow."

As I joined her on the journey to the ICU, we passed rooms with monitoring equipment and IV bags attached to the patients. Suddenly, the severity of her condition hit me. I gently stretched over the side rails of her bed, kissing her softly. "The doctor wants to keep you here and get to the bottom of this. He says you have an infection in the pancreas."

Her eyes narrowed thoughtfully "They have to fix it."

"Yes, yes they will."

I only half believed it myself. The doctor's warning that she would be sick didn't give me much confidence in the outcome.

"Mr. Phillips, I'm Jane, the charge nurse. You have to go to the waiting room and give us time to get your wife settled. I'll come and get you when she's ready."

"Okay, take care of her please."

Walking out of the room I suddenly felt a dry burning in my throat and tears welling up. This is where people come to die. I took one deep breath. Get a grip on yourself. How will I raise my kids without her? Did I cause this? Did I give her an ulcer of the pancreas? Is that even possible?

I called Dottie from the phone booth in the waiting room.

"Hi, mom" before I could say anything she let out a barrage of questions.

"Hold on, I'll tell you everything. She has something called pancreatitis. They admitted her. We'll know more tomorrow after more tests."

Knowing her nervous condition, I deliberately left out the ICU, and just told her she was on the second floor.

Jane came to get me. "She is resting comfortably. We started some IVs. She will probably go to sleep soon and rest through the night. Would you like to see her now?"

Jane walked with me past the nurses' station, and to her room. I wondered why she stayed by my side until I caught sight of all the medical paraphernalia. If the amount of equipment was any measure of the seriousness of the illness, Carol was indeed very sick, just as the doctor had said.

The next day, Dr. DeAngelis, a tall, slender, rather good-looking surgeon, introduced himself to me, explaining once again that my wife was "a very sick girl." I wondered if that was a phrase they learned in med school. "Very sick girl. Very sick boy."

"She's running a high temperature, that's a sign of the heavy infection. We need to open her up and find out what's going on inside."

I was at his mercy, trusting him to know exactly what he was doing. I gave my permission for an exploratory of the abdomen. Sensing my nervousness, he tried to comfort me. With his hand on my shoulder, he said, "We'll do all we can."

There was something about the way he said that. It resonated in my head. Did he believe she was beyond help? She was taken to the OR moments later, before my in-laws arrived. I knew I would catch hell for that, not that I was in control of the Operating Room schedule.

They had no sooner arrived when Dr. De Angelis came out in his scrubs. He explained that he found a large infection in the pancreas, and the gallbladder was inflamed. While I was not sure of everything he told us, Dottie just could not get enough information. I am sure the doctor would have loved to walk away, but he showed a tremendous amount of patience and understanding.

He explained that the pancreas is a gland about six inches long, behind the stomach, that secretes pancreatic juices, digestive enzymes, insulin, and glucose into the duodenum. He might as well have been speaking a foreign language. Nonetheless, I was appreciative that he took the time to explain. He told us Carol would be in recovery for a couple of hours and we should go get some breakfast.

We sat in the snack bar, digesting the information, and forming more questions. What causes pancreatitis? What will be the long-term consequences? The longer we sat there, the more questions we had. Sitting across the table from her, I studied Dottie. Normally, an extremely nervous person, now even more so. She had a consistent 'tell' when she was nervous. She would sniffle; short, consecutive sniffles and then pass her index finger under her nostrils, for no purpose. Today, with each sniffle, her index finger came with a slight heaving from the chest. In any other setting it might have been embarrassing but not during all the emotional upheaval. To distract her I asked, "What do you think of Dr. D?"

She replied, "He can put his shoes under my bed any time."

That statement left a lasting impression, it was the first and last time I ever heard her engage in anything remotely comical or with any sexual connotation. It was well after noon when the nurse entered the waiting room.

"Mr. Phillips, you may come in and visit for a while. Your wife will probably be sleeping, Only two at a time, please."

"Come on, mom. Let's go in."

We entered the room; the sight was a shock to the system. My mother-in-law went weak in the knees and the nurse helped her out of the room and administered some smelling salts. The scent of disinfectant invaded my nostrils, I felt like a kite caught in a strong wind, tattered and uncontrollable. The paraphernalia of yesterday failed by comparison to post-surgery. I took in the IV pole supporting the bags of fluids and blood. Surgical tubes were protruding from under the blankets, terminating in plastic bags half full of dark blood and urine. Next to the bed was a machine with two glass cylinders encasing two accordion-type bellows, each one inflating and deflating with a swish and hissing sound in perfect cadence with her breathing.

Suddenly, the bellows went silent. Breathless, petrified, and powerless, I turned. It started again. I navigated my way to the bedside, gently reached over the respiratory hose pulsating from the tracheotomy. I touched her soft face, still and lifeless. I thought of how, in past times, my touch could generate heat and vibrant responses. Today, the flushed face and burning eyes were mine. My mother-in-law had returned to the room, standing next to me, pale and trembling. I took her into my arms, silently, as the tears rolled down our faces.

There was no obvious change over the next couple of days. Carol was non- responsive. Dottie and I kept bedside vigil as a parade of doctors, nurses, and specialists passed through several times a day. In addition to pulmonary specialists and technicians, there was Dr. Chaudhry and, of course, Dr. De Angelis. Dr. D talked with me every day but did not have anything good to say. Carol was still running a temperature and had an infection that was not responding to medication. On day five, he explained why it was necessary to go back in.

One day post-surgery, Dr. Chaudhry took me aside and told me I should prepare her family and our children for the eventuality that she was not going to make it. His bluntness caught me off guard. "She is going to die." Simple as that, and then he left, just as quickly as he had arrived.

Later, when Dr. De Angelis arrived, I told him of the conversation.

"Larry, the Indian doctors have seen a lot of death and dying, and their bedside manner is kind of cold. But in all fairness, I must tell you things don't look good. However, I have also seen a lot of miracles. You should keep your faith and pray."

Later that day, when I arrived for my afternoon visit, I overheard two nurses talking about Dr. D's heroic action in reviving a patient. The patient had been Carol. It had been a tough day. One doctor told me she was going to die, and the other advised me to pray. Two nurses said. "She already died and came back."

****

There were days when I drove the 22-mile round-trip to the hospital three times, then drove fifty miles into work. There were nights when I would sneak into the hospital, through the emergency room, up to ICU, just checking in to see how she was doing.

Those days, I would go home, skip the morning visit, and get the boys off to school. That would be followed by a couple of hours of sleep before the afternoon visit. My father had come to stay with us. Between him and my in-laws, there was always somebody home with the kids. It was not an easy time for anyone, we all made sacrifices. My boys sacrificed the most, unable to see their mother. They were not old enough to visit in the hospital, not that I wanted them to see her in her current condition.

She was gradually losing her hair. The doctors explained it was from the medicine and in time would reverse itself, oddly enough, it was growing on her face. Carol was still not showing any signs of improvement it was decided another surgery would be necessary to remove the stones from the gallbladder duct. That surgery lasted six hours, and waited on edge, every minute, looking for Dr. D to return from the OR.

It was October before she started to show signs of improvement. They removed the breathing machine and eventually closed the tracheotomy. Gradually, some of the intravenous tubing was removed and she was started on soft foods and ice chips.

November was slightly better, but we had all agreed not to mention Thanksgiving. When we turned the calendar page to December, Christmas was on everyone's mind. I started consulting with the doctors, hoping they would agree to a discharge before the holidays. The consensus was "wait and see." They encouraged us not to get too excited, because anything could happen, and once again, we should "keep the faith."

As the staff spoke of her leaving the ICU and going to a stepdown unit, the excitement built in both the family and the staff. We were entering the fourth month in ICU. December was a month full of therapy; physical, respiratory, speech, and occupational. It was clear the doctors and staff were all working to make her our Christmas present for 1974.

I remember the day Carol asked for a mirror. With fear and trepidation, I handed it to her.

Her first reaction was, "That's not me! That's not me!"

It took only a minute for her to realize that it was indeed her. She became silent for a little while, reconciling herself to the loss of hair on her head and the growth on her face. I told her it was temporary and that her appearance was the least of our problems. We had to get her strong enough to go home. Her lips curled slowly into a smile. It had been a long time since I had seen her smile. And whose fault was that I asked myself over and over.

She was given a tentative release window of Christmas week. I knew once she got home, my time was not going to be my own. I planned to get a night for myself but not by myself. I called the

19-year-old and told everyone I was going to work. Returning my date to her house, after a night of dancing and drinking, I pulled up at a stop light next to Charlie and Dottie. By the time I realized it was them, I was in his blind spot. Our steering wheels were eighteen inches from parallel. If he glanced to his left, he would be face to face with my chosen pleasure of the evening. Suddenly, it was as if I had swallowed a fist full of jalapeno peppers. I had violated the major rule of serial cheaters "Don't shit where you eat, or you wind up eating shit." The light changed and neither car moved for what seemed an eternity. I thought for sure he knew it was me and that he was just waiting for me to pull ahead. Finally, he pulled away. I slowly moved and made the next left, not knowing if I had been made or not. What the hell are they doing out early on Sunday morning? Could they be on their way to the hospital? Had she taken a turn for the worse? Were they called because I wasn't reachable? I had to suppress the nausea that I was feeling.

A wave of guilt swept over me. You selfish, stupid jerk. Was a piece of ass and some music worth it? I always felt remorse after I screwed up; when she went into the psychiatric hospital, when I went on the three-day bender with Miss Big Breasts, and all the countless times that had gone undetected. Now as she may be taking her last breath, I was heavy breathing with a 19-year-old.

17. Home From the Hospital

The ambulance rolled down West End Avenue and backed onto our black top driveway. Linda Harris, part of the volunteer ambulance crew, was middle-aged, approximately 140 to 150 pounds, with a streaky blond ponytail. She moved with smooth professionalism and had a genuine caring attitude. She showed the utmost attention to Carol, making sure she was settled and comfortable. As they were leaving, I offered them a donation.

"We can't take it, but you could drop it at the garage during the week."

"Well, then Merry Christmas and thank you very much. I appreciate your coming out on Christmas Eve."

"Not at all, we're happy for you and hope your wife's recovery is swift and complete. In the meantime, you behave yourself and do the right thing."

"You bet," I replied automatically.

All the holiday wishes having been said, I watched as the ambulance pulled out of the driveway.

The family's excitement level was high. With nervous anticipation, the boys and I gathered at Carol's bedside.

"Well, honey, welcome home. How does it feel to be back in your bed?"

Nervously she said, "I don't know I, don't..."

"You're the greatest Christmas present we ever had." I interrupted.

It became clear that she was uncomfortable without the 24/7 medical staff. We had a long talk, where I did my best to convince her that the visiting nurse and physical therapist would take care of her and report back both to Dr. De Angelis and Dr. Chaudhry.

I had taken two weeks' vacation so that I could be home day and night. The chores were never ending; shopping, cooking, kids to school, cleaning, etc.

By the spring of 1975, I had realized that mothers and homemakers should have a 20-year retirement program.

One day, after completing my errands, I stopped at the volunteer ambulance squad garage to donate and to let those in charge know how pleased I was with the job they had done. I especially wanted to acknowledge Linda Harris, who had been so caring and pleasant.

The gentleman who accepted the check said, "Who?"

"Linda Harris." I continued to describe how attentive she had been. I even remembered her final remarks about doing the right thing.

He shrugged, "No Harris here, but thank you for the donation."

On the short drive home, I thought how strange and yet relevant. She had advised me to "do the right thing" and now she was nowhere to be found. I'll have to stop back again another day. I'm not crazy.

***

Carol's dressings had to be changed by the visiting nurse, but I often inspected for signs of infection between visits. Day by day her strength improved, and she spent more time out of bed than in it. Although it zapped what energy she had, it was a wonderful sight the first time she ate her dinner at the kitchen table.

When the day arrived for her scheduled appointment with Dr. D, I called to explain that she couldn't get around all that well. He told me that we could come to the back door and he would get us in and out quickly.

The back door opened and Dr. D was genuinely pleased with Carol's obvious progress.

He called for Jenny, the scrub nurse who had assisted in Carol's surgeries. "Jenny, call upstairs. Tell Dr. Chaudhry I need him for a second."

As Chaudhry entered, "Hey Rojas, look at this!"

"Mrs. Phillips, you have come a long way. How are you feeling?"

"Better every day, but still very weak."

With a "Keep up the good work," he scampered back to his office. He seemed annoyed that his prophecy had not been fulfilled.

18. Flipping Pancakes to Pay Bills

The International House of Pancakes was building a new restaurant in downtown Brentwood. If I could get a morning shift there, I could end the afternoon traffic jam. I applied and was hired, after a short pre-opening training program, as opening lead cook. Not only did I get a job, but I also arranged to have two early days at the News. So I worked five days and had no overlapping schedule. I gave notice at the Bow Wow and was told if I ever wanted to return, they would have a place for me.

By this time the medical bills had been processed by the insurance companies and many unpaid balances were arriving daily. I began receiving collection calls from the providers. I explained the length of the hospital stay and that I needed time. I had a regular spiel for everyone who called that always concluded with the fact that I intended to pay my debts. The calls that came from collection agencies were less understanding and more threatening. Their demands came as letters with red ink, or with obvious large print return address labels. In the months that followed, I paid off most of the bills, the smaller ones first.

When I received a call from Mr. Hope (probably not his real name), from an agency representing Good Samaritan Hospital, I gave him my usual spiel, but he interrupted me rudely claiming that I hadn't made any effort to pay my $7000 debt and that they demanded immediate payment, in full.

I was indignant. "I have paid off thousands of dollars in medical bills. You have no idea what I have done. I work two full-time jobs to meet my responsibilities."

Interrupting again, he said, "I know you work for the Daily News."

"Where I work is none of your business and if you interrupt me again this conversation is over. I don't have $7,000."

"Can you borrow it from your family?"

"No, the hospital can easily afford to absorb the loss of $7,000 or take payments. As a matter of fact, the hospital wrote it off when they gave it to you."

"That doesn't matter, you haven't made an effort to pay anything."

That made my blood boil. "You son of a bitch, you're just a parasite feeding on the downtrodden and less fortunate. If you were here, I'd grab you by the throat and squeeze the life out of you."

"You want to meet me? Come to my office. I'll see you face-to-face."

"Say when." I roared.

"Tomorrow at 1 p.m.?"

"See you then, Mr. Hope."

When I hung up, Carol said, "Are you nuts? You can't threaten him."

"Well, I did, didn't I? I'll go see him tomorrow."

"Then I'll go with you."

"I can't take a woman to fight my battles. Besides you're out of shape."

We half smiled and I hugged her. "Hey, you're starting to firm up maybe I'll take you for moral support."

We sat in a small waiting room with only three chairs, and a receptionist visible through a glass window next to a solid door that clicked locked after each person entered. They must get a lot of threats. We sat quietly, waiting to be called. One man started to stand up from behind his desk and just keep getting up. He must have been six-something with shoulders to be measured with a yardstick. After he exited the office, through the waiting room, I said I hoped he wasn't Mr. Hope.

We laughed until he returned, "Mr. and Mrs. Phillips would you like to come inside?"

We sat in the straight office chairs next to his desk. I nervously set my briefcase on my lap. This was the case I had used to smuggle six bottles of wine out of the St. Regis wine cellar almost every day.

"Tell me what's been going on. Let's see if we can come to a resolution."

"I have all my bills, the ones I paid and the ones still outstanding."

As I unfastened the snap lock, the case was upside down and all its contents spilled out on the floor next to his desk. I scrambled to recover everything and apologized at the same time.

"That's quite a pile of bills. You weren't kidding, were you?" He quipped.

"No, perhaps now you can understand a little better."

"This is marked paid, this is paid, this one, too," as he helped pick up the invoices and handed them to me.

"I have each company or doctor stapled together, and here is a tally sheet listing the payee with the amount and date. The rest are unpaid and pending, like yours."

"Mr. and Mrs. Phillips, I'm sorry for your situation. And you were right, we buy the account from the hospital. But we have to recover some amount to stay in business."

"Mr. Hope, what can I do? I have a decent income, of course, with two jobs. It should be enough, but with all this debt..."

"Mr. Phillips, can you give me $2000 in a lump sum?"

"Then what?"

"Then you're done, were even. Paid in full."

The man I wanted to choke to death was now my new $5,000 friend.

"Let me see what I can do, give me a few days and I'll call you."

Once more, I was depending on my in-laws for the $2000, having explained that I saved us five grand. It was a no-interest loan that I paid off in about two months. I continued to make myself available for all the overtime I could handle.

I still had an obligation of $3000 to Dr. DeAngelis. The better part of the year had passed and I wanted to do something nice for him. Of course, he wanted for nothing, so I thought I'd pay him off the books. His statements came every month but never with red type or past-due notices. I put the cash in an envelope and took it with me on Carol's next office visit. As we were leaving, I offered him the envelope.

Puzzled he said, "What's up?"

"I want you to know that of all the bills for Carol's illness, yours was the only one that never went to a collection agency, never typed in red, not one phone call. I have paid off everyone. It took time, but I'm proud to say I've done it. Yours is the last one."

He took the envelope, "Cash is nice but I've got too many partners."

"I thought maybe you and your wife could get away for a weekend."

"How much is in here?"

"Our balance of $3,000. It's because you never hounded me like all the rest."

"Larry, I never get involved with the billing, The girls take care of all of that."

"I just wanted you to know I appreciate all you have done."

He set the envelope down, we shook hands and with a chorus of "thank yous," ended our visit.

***

Carol started attending a weekly Bible study with some of the neighbor ladies. That was something I avoided like the plague. One evening it was Carol's turn to host and I positioned myself for a quick getaway then I heard, "Wives be in submission to your husbands." That, I thought, came just at the right time in my marriage.

"Wives be in submission to your husbands. Is that in the Bible?" I asked.

"Yes, Ephesians 5:22. The Bible is the manufacturer's handbook. Everything you need to know is in here."

This was my introduction to Howard Style and his wife Ruth. Howard was about 60 years old, soft-spoken, gentle, and well educated; not only in the Bible but church history and Christianity in general.

I had been in submission to her for a while. I took the apartment across the street from her parents. When we moved to the house in Brentwood, I didn't object to her parents moving across the street. I took the kids to church. I stood by her throughout her illness. I had worked two jobs during our entire marriage. I worked hard on our relationship and...

I was suddenly shaken out of my self-pity trance when Howard's soft voice expounded, "Husbands love your wives as Christ so loved the church." Still attentive, of course Christ loves the church.

"We are his church" Howard explained. "The followers of Jesus Christ are his church."

Okay, I'm not stupid. I get it. The people are the church, the church is the people.

The Bible teacher exclaimed, "Jesus loves the church, the people, you and me, so much he died for us." Continuing softly, "Husbands, do you love your wives enough to die for them? Are you Christlike in your marriage?"

The question was searing, to say the least. Would I die for her? Sometimes I wanted to kill her, not literally, but angry enough to walk out and slam the door.

By the time I had driven halfway to the News, I realized how unfair I was to even think I had reason to be unhappy with her. With all that I had put her through, I knew I had to be somewhat responsible for her physical and psychological condition.

I continued to go to the Bible studies when I could and if it was convenient. At one session, we had a guest. Bob, who played guitar and sang gospel songs, gave testimony to his Christian conversion. I listened as he enthusiastically shared what others were witnessing to him about Jesus.

"Jesus, Jesus, Jesus." he went on to say. "I had enough Jesus to last a lifetime. And that night when I went to bed, I said *Jesus, if you're real, you'll have to call and tell me.* In that instant, the phone rang." Bob claimed that he shook nervously and broke into a sweat as he placed the receiver to his ear. "Hello." On the other end, someone said, "Bob, I just wanted to tell you Jesus loves you." And from that moment on, he had never been the same person.

That night was one of the most pleasant Bible studies I ever attended. The lesson was good, the witnessing was good, Bob's music was good. Perhaps some people came into my life for a reason, I didn't always know the reason, but I was starting to think, perhaps they were the angels.

Howard mentioned Hebrews 13 "Some have entertained angels unawares." *Holy cow! Linda Harris, Bob, and how many others who had tried to introduce me to Jesus?*

Carol often talked about having seen a bright light in one of the times she stopped breathing. Not an out-of-body experience, but a very bright light. More than a few times she expressed that "God must've saved her for something special."

Don't misunderstand, my return to the church was not an overnight bolt of lightning experience and God knows I often strayed. I increased my knowledge of the Bible, often questioning the Trinity, the New Testament, the Old Testament, and who wrote the Bible. I didn't remember any of this from Catholic school.

In time, with little reminders, my behavior started to change. Smoking, drinking, foul language, and extra-marital exploits were rare. One Sunday sermon contained the statement, "If you want the Holy Spirit in your life, you can't drown him in booze and choke him in smoke!" That day, I smoked my last cigar. God also knows I didn't go from sinner to saint. That journey was still underway, but I started to develop a conscience. It is difficult for me to describe what was going on in my life. I knew when I was doing something wrong but did it anyway. There was a spiritual war being waged and the Holy Spirit often lost to the pull of the world. Howard had been right. The manufacturer's handbook became more interesting. I even bought one of my own and Howard became my spiritual father. One may refer to me as a baby in the Lord. I could sometimes talk the talk, but to walk the walk, not so much.

***

My return to Madison Square Garden was neither to work nor steal, but to be worked on. Howard and Ruth knew of the preacher, David Wilkinson, who had founded Teen Challenge, an inter-city youth group. Reverend Wilkinson was holding a one-night crusade at the Garden and Howard suggested some members of the Bible study group attend. I thought it would be good for my boys and so we made plans to attend as a family. I just happened to have a recorder I had boosted from the audiovisual room at the high school. So, I returned to the scene of an earlier crime with evidence of a second crime, to listen to the word of God and illegally record some of the Christian music.

Wilkerson had a great following. He had been the main character, played by Pat Boone, in a movie called "The Cross and the Switchblade." People arrived by busloads. The music was good and the preaching was dynamic. He was a show in and of himself. I was impressed with the extemporaneous way he preached. His message was from the book of Revelation. I was so impressed with the whole night, I played the recording over and over to better understand the message. I was also quick to share it with others.

The lesson had been about being lukewarm, neither hot nor cold, and how God would spit you out if you were lukewarm. This invokes imagery of lukewarm water turning one's stomach and causing one to vomit. It can be interpreted to mean that lukewarm Christians made him sick. By spitting them out, he is rejecting those who can't decide whether to follow him or not.

Revelation 3:16, NIV: "So, because you are lukewarm--neither hot nor cold--I am about to spit you out of my mouth."

I certainly learned well because "lukewarm" and "spit" began to reverberate in my mind every time temptation came knocking.

19. Knock, Knock

"Behold, I stand at the door, and knock: if any man hears my voice, and opens the door, I will come into him and will sup with him, and he with me." Rev 3:20

Joe was on again, off again, with drugs, beer, and Jesus when he introduced me to Pastor Hair of Calvary Baptist Church. The pastor was a short stocky man with the typical dark suit and liturgical collar. His few short strands of hair on each side, just above the ears, made his name unforgettable. The introduction included an invite to Sunday service and a home visit.

Shortly after, I was invited to a three-day crusade at his church. There were speakers from Jerry Falwell's Liberty Baptist College (now University). Dr. H. L. Wilmington, a professor at the college, had written: "Willmington's Guide to the Bible." The three-inch-thick reference book outlined the chronological method and the theological approach to studying the word of God. The autographed copy is still in my library to this day.

The sermons and evangelical preaching during the crusade centered around how you must be "born again," a new term to me. John 3:5 states "Very truly I tell you, no one can enter the kingdom of God unless they are born of water and the Spirit." Soon I realized that when you draw closer to Jesus and the Holy

Spirit, the devil himself becomes manifest. The pull of the world, and all I thought to be normal and acceptable, was drawn into a spiritual war. I had second thoughts on many things. Knock, Knock!

***

It was early spring on Long Island. Robert was a high school freshman, anxious to play football and lacrosse and I was still at IHOP, fed up with pancakes and eggs. I answered an ad for a day-time truck driver position at a local nursery; no loading, just driving. That fit me, no manual labor. I drove out to the farm in East Port, Long Island, almost every day to pick up a truckload of trees and plant material. Sometimes I would load extras and drop them off at my house, on the way to the Huntington nursery. I did that for a year, landscaping the house and planting evergreens on both sides of the driveway. Between driving the truck and flipping newspapers at the Roto, my days were full and exhausting.

***

One night at the paper, the office boy came out to the press, "Phillips, call home. No rush."

Carol was upset and anxious. There was nothing specific wrong, but she wanted me to come home. Sensing the urgency in her voice and concerned by her past suicidal thoughts, I got someone to cover for me and headed home.

I picked up a six-pack of Budweiser before getting on the Long Island Expressway and by the time I had reached the Nassau County line it was raining lightly, enough to put a sheen on the blacktop, and I had finished three beers. Fighting to stay awake, I checked the time. Almost 3 a.m. Suddenly, a thump, and I was veering left off into the next lane. My car spun around, and head-lights were now bearing down on me. Fear and panic set in. I had no control of the 67 Impala as I stiff-legged the brake to the floor causing deep ruts as it rolled backward down the median and came to a stop.

I sat for a moment, calming my rapidly beating heart. I exited the car and walked up to the roadway, illuminated by the head-lights of the cars that had stopped.

"Did you hit me?" I asked the driver of a fuel oil tanker.

"No, you hit him," pointing down the road to a second tanker that was parked on the shoulder with its emergency flashers blinking.

"And then you hit that Mustang." That car had front-end damage on the right side.

The Suffolk County Highway Patrol arrived and found that there were no personal injuries. The driver of the lead truck said that I must have bounced off his tires. I admitted that I was tired and most likely had fallen asleep at the wheel. No one, including the driver of the Mustang (an off-duty police officer), questioned anything further. I had dodged a bullet on several fronts. There had been no injuries, no breathalyzer, and I supposed the officer had not wanted to slosh through the mud to examine my car, where he would have found the evidence that I had been drinking while driving.

I let out a sigh of relief when I pulled into my driveway. I sat there for a few minutes until I began to nod off. I pulled myself out of the car and up the front steps. The house was dark and quiet. Carol had fallen asleep, but I knew I had to wake her to tell her about the damage to the car.

Groggily she said, "Oh, I waited and waited."

"I had an accident."

"An accident? What kind of accident?"

"With the car, it's banged up pretty bad."

"How did it happen?"

"I hit a truck full of gasoline."

"How the hell did you do that?"

"I fell asleep."

"Why didn't you pull over and rest?

"Because I was concerned… forget it, I just wanted to tell you before you saw it yourself."

I started to disrobe, wet jacket, muddy shoes, and work clothes, as Carol got out of bed to check on the damage to the car.

The next morning I woke up early, annoyed at myself for the accident and angry at Carol because she seemed to only be concerned about the car. She hadn't asked if I was hurt or if anyone else was. Someone could have been fried to a crisp if the fuel tanker had exploded. But the only thing on her mind was the cost to repair the car.

I spent the rest of the day stewing about everything; paper, pancakes, and plant material. Until I realized those were the things that supported my family. I should just thank God that no one had been hurt and that I had not been arrested for DWI. Knock! Knock!

***

In our ten years at the Brentwood house, we became friendly with the couple across the street. Bill and Pickles owned and operated a cesspool business, both cleaning, and installation of either block or precast pools. Bill would go out with the pumper while Pickles handled the phone. When they decided to expand the construction part, they needed to hire a driver for the pumper, and I was offered the job. It was not labor-intensive, but it's fair (more than fair) to say most days it stunk.

The job did, however, inspire the following verse:

As a father with two young boys
Offered a position for part-time employ,
Drive a truck? I'll get off my rump.
1,000-gallon tank and a vacuum pump.

Clean a cesspool, that's something new.
I've made a commitment, I'll stand true.
Drag the four-inch poly hose,
Three inches wet grass, easy to diagnose.

Soft soil swishes over heels and soles.
Remove this slab, expose the hole.
Sudden relief, ghastly fluids gush free,
Acid fumes ascend the nasal cavities.

Staring down into the abyss, my skin is itchy.
Murky, turbid waters, feces of varied viscosity.
Voracious hose sucks semi-solids of shapes and shades,
Circling the straw like a leaf in cascades.

1,000 gallons later, plumbing is dignified.
This job is well done, my ride is curbside.
Rear bumper could be read,
Your poop is my butter and bread

***

The midnight Roto had always been a good job. It was mostly straight time, except for clean-up on Saturday morning. After making some inquiries, I learned I could make big money if I transferred downstairs to the "black." That is how they referred to the daily paper because it was only printed in black ink at that time. There I would get 2-1/2 hours of overtime per shift and work with partners, which would allow me to go home early every other night. My ten years of experience qualified me for spotting the plates (putting them in page order). They were made of lead and weighed 42 pounds each.

I hooked up with a reliable and conscientious partner. He didn't drink, play cards, or leave his workstation. The money started to roll in and every other night I was home early, often before the presses started. Many nights there was post-shift overtime, as well. These shenanigans were a common practice, but if you ask anyone, they will deny it. All the bosses were promoted from within the ranks, so they did the same thing before becoming a boss. On top of all that, Saturday morning was available at the New York Times on 43rd Street in Manhattan and they opened a plant in Carlstadt, New Jersey. The three shifts always afforded work opportunities, any day, any shift. That was all the work I wanted or could handle. It meant the end of part-time jobs, but we were spending it as fast as I made it.

***

Carol and I were told about a new preacher who was starting a church in Central Islip. The old chapel was in a graveyard and was falling apart. Uneven and broken floorboards, chipped paint, and loose and broken pews were just a few of its problems. The only thing that didn't need help was the preacher. David K. Fox, a young man in good shape, was a Florida Bible School graduate.

Accompanying him were his wife and in-laws, all working together to establish this new church. Week after week the attendance grew, as did the collection plate. David was a sincere, powerful speaker. When asked what I thought of him, I would say, "Someday he'll be a great preacher."

Six years later, David announced he had saved enough money to secure a loan for a piece of property at Motor Parkway and Wheeler Road. Soon after, he led us in a march around the parcel of land, claiming it in the name of the Lord as had been done at the walls of Jericho. Knowing of my thirst for knowledge, he informed me of a Bible school in Oyster Bay run by the Assembly of God, a Pentecostal denomination. Before long, I was attending classes there on my way home from work. This lasted the better part of a year, padding the payroll at night and praising the Lord in the morning. Knock! Knock! Knock!

***

Our Bible study group had grown until it was an ecumenical assembly; Presbyterian, Baptist, Lutheran, Catholic, and us, now the Church of God (Pentecostal.)

Some of the couples were going on a weekend retreat in Bay Shore, Long Island, and Carol and I were invited. Not revealing any details, I was encouraged to trust my fellow Christians and step out in faith. I agreed and embarked on Tres Dias (Spanish for three days.) The event was held in the Catholic seminary, now used exclusively as a retreat house. It was a structured program that started with introductions and instructions on Thursday. Friday morning was low-key, with Saturday becoming more intense. By Sunday, I had experienced three days of teaching, sharing, praying, and singing.

I took part in many weekends, in different roles, such as table leader, kitchen help, or speaker on several topics. Before long I was tapped as rector for Tres Dias #19. The rector had the job of planning, organizing, staffing, reviewing all talks, and holding weekly meetings with the team. Without divulging all the details, Tres Dias #19 was the best! Men were moved, families changed, confessions were made, and souls were rejuvenated. Three years later, an older man, Martin, who had attended #19, pulled me aside to tell me that I had changed his life forever that weekend.

"What was it?"

He replied, "A sin is a sin, no matter what shape it's in."

"Martin," I said, "God allowed man to sin so that he might display his grace. As Paul wrote in Romans 5:20, 'Where sin abounded, grace did much more abound.' Do you think God is up in heaven keeping the list of bad words and tallying how many times we say each one? Maybe, but I don't think so. I think God is more offended when we participate in gossip, ungrateful talking, racist and sexist talk, and class talk." As his eyes started to glisten, we shared an embrace.

***

The Tres Dias weekends and the weekly Bible studies continued. Growth and blessings came in abundance. I became involved in the opening of a Christian bookstore in Brentwood. It was a sweat equity arrangement with a widow from the Bible study group. Leasing, opening, stocking, and running the store was a great experience. However, sales did not generate enough revenue to meet the overhead and it soon closed.

20. Schools

In the summer of 1975, I started working at Brentwood High School as part of a new security program, the forerunner for today's school resource officers.

Ed Franchi, Assistant Dean, had been saddled with organizing a pilot program. It was understood, that if it failed the employees would be terminated along with the program. The prerequisites were few. You had to be a Brentwood resident, physically fit, have a valid driver's license, and pass a background check.

The twelve new hires were to be trained by four off-duty detectives from the Third Precinct of the Suffolk County Police Department. Instruction included misdemeanors and felonies, searches and pat-downs, handcuffs (our only tool of enforcement), compliance techniques, and radio procedures. Our walkie-talkies put us in direct contact with Franchi who had a base station on his desk.

The program started in two high school buildings, the Ross and the Sonderling, later expanding to a district-wide program. The Brentwood School District covered twenty-two square miles and twenty buildings. The operation was 24/7 and included radio patrol cars and dispatches. The expansion came with a supervisory title and a radio installed in my car. I also became the voice of the program, speaking at PTA meetings.

Louis Rodriguez, Isaac James, and I were assigned to the day-shift at the Ross building because our ethnic makeup closely fit with that of the students. It was not long before the kids had nick-named us "the mick, the spic, and the spook." We chose to ignore it and we got along well with each other. Isaac talked basketball with the boys, Louis spoke Spanish, and I tried to build relation-ships with everyone. When some kids were found to have pot in their possession and the word traveled fast that we were friendly but not their friend.

***

When construction started on the Blue Ridge condos in Med-ford, they were advertised as golfdominiums. It was condo living with a clubhouse, indoor and outdoor swimming pools, and a nine-hole golf course. This appealed to me. I visited several times and each time it looked better and better. I mulled it over almost daily, with "what if" questions running through my head. What if the developer ran out of money? What if the common charges became too high? What if I wait to commit until it was built out? Would it then cost more?

Dottie and Charlie's advancing age made the idea of condo liv-ing appealing to them, too. We continued to weigh the pros and cons, and three years later all three families, the grandparents, both daughters and husbands, and five grandchildren, moved to Medford.

Robert was in his senior year when we moved, and he wanted to graduate with his class. He had a car, an old Buick gifted to him by Richie Freebs, so we allowed him to commute the ten miles from our new home to his old school. No skin off my nose, right? All true until the school caught on and we had to pay "out of district" tuition. Charles was just starting high school and was happy to enroll in the Patchogue-Medford district.

Robert was advancing in football but also was an excellent, super-fast, lacrosse midfielder.

Charles took up wrestling and I soon realized the character de-velopment that was gained through a one-on-one sport. Wrestling taught Chuck to accept both the victories and defeats with grace. One day, after a crushing loss, he sat against the bleachers with his head in his hands. I approached, trying to be of some comfort, but he waved me off saying, "He beat me fair and square."

We were thrilled with our new home. I learned to play golf, we bought all new modern furniture, I painted large graphic designs on the walls that were reflected in the wall-to-wall mirrors, and the move only added ten miles each way to my commute.

Weekends offered us time to experience golf at the short, par-three course. We gathered an arm full of clubs and headed to the tee box. We must have been a sight because everyone offered unsolicited help. I never realized there were so many "golf pros" offering free lessons or perhaps they just wanted us off the greens and out of the way. The boys were always well-behaved and respectful; reserving their comments until we got home.

After one semester at Suffolk Community College, Robert asked if we would take him on a weekend visit to VMI?

"Wear and what is a VMI?"

"It's the West Point of the south."

"How far south?"

He hesitated. "Virginia. Is that too far?"

Virginia. That was my destination when I attempted to run away with Dennis Cox. Was Robert trying to get out of the house and get away?

"Too far, Dad?"

"No, no that's cool. When? Get me some info!"

It was midsummer 1983 when the four of us piled into the VW bug. The weekend visit was an opportunity for Robert to taste life at the military school and to see if it felt right for him, before committing. The school had already agreed to accept his credits from Suffolk.

Most of the trip was highway and turnpike until we reached Virginia and the Blue Ridge Mountains. The Blue Ridge Parkway's picturesque landscape was absolutely beautiful. The scenery was the only thing that kept Carol's mind off the idea of her baby going 500 miles away to school.

When we arrived, we were greeted by two uniformed cadets who assured us that Robert would be in good hands for the weekend. They asked if we needed directions to the Key-Det Motel and said, "We'll see you Sunday, 1600 hours, Mr. and Mrs. Phillips. It was a pleasure meeting you." After handshakes, we hesitantly walked back to the car wondering what they were going to do with our baby.

Sunday afternoon, Robert was returned to us, as promised. We had not even pulled away from the curb when he said, "This is where I want to go to school."

"What makes you so sure?"

"Dad, it's the discipline! I'll learn here. Suffolk is just an extension of high school."

"Are you sure? It was only one weekend."

"I know, but I did a lot and I saw a lot. I got an overall view of what it's like here."

Carol mused forlornly and said, "If you're sure, and you do sound sure, I guess it's okay."

"There is one other thing," Bob said. "The first semester is $5000, due in August, before matriculation. Oh, and no visitors until Parents' Weekend."

"When is that?" Carol asked.

"After the first ten weeks. It's a big deal... a parade and all."

"I can't see my baby for ten weeks?"

"No, Mom, and stop calling me your baby."

As we pushed the VW over the hills and highways it became obvious that we would also need a better, more comfortable car if we were going to make this trip regularly.

***

My sister, Grace, and her husband, Bob, were the most entertaining and hospitable couple I had ever known. They hosted the best get-togethers, barbecues, Christmases, and beach parties. For many years, they leased a house directly on the beach in Sag Harbor, Long Island, and extended an open invitation to the entire family and beyond. Often Marilyn would rent the house next to it and sometimes Cousin Loretta took the third house. The uniform for the weekend was always bathing suits.

Clams were caught by day and consumed each evening in the flickering light of the campfires. Richie, from the Bow Wow, was an expert at opening clams, and Grace made a killer clam chowder. I remember one late August, the flames faded to a blue bed of ash and the moon's reflection spread across the inflatable beach toys at the edge of the lapping water. One by one, everyone crashed, some in sleeping bags on the beach. Several tents were fully occupied by children. A few adults still sat sipping their beverage of choice.

My cousin, Veronica, and I were sitting on a retaining wall, reminiscing about the old days in the Bronx when I used to visit with my mother. I was impressed with how attractive she had become, reminding her of her skinny adolescence and her short platinum hair.

"Oh yeah, how about you, four eyes? And the suspenders and your hair plastered flat to your head."

"Touché," as we laughed into the night air.

We continued our conversation, sharing some of the rocky moments in our former and current relationships, finding we had much in common. Realizing how late it was, we decided to turn in before the sun came up. "Good night, cuz. Thanks for being so open, and for the sentimental journey back to the old neighborhood." A bubble of laughter rose in her throat.

***

While perusing the used car lot, Carol's suddenly declared, "I like that one. The white one. I like how it looks."

"It's a Lincoln!"

"So?"

"So, it's not cheap."

"I like that one and I want it," she said, totally out of character. It didn't take much to convince me. That day we went from a Volkswagen bug to a signature series Lincoln Town Car.

***

As we motored down the highway toward VMI "How's the ride back there?" I asked.

"Sure beats the bug."

"Are you nervous, Bob?"

"I think I know what to expect. They showed us a film about Rat Week it's a lot of harassment. Everyone gets a haircut and you get loaded down with all your equipment and your hay."

Chuck asked, "What's hay?"

"It's your mattress."

"What the heck, you sleep on the floor?"

"No, everyone gets a new mattress and you keep it for the next four years."

The conversation went on for many miles with Carol occasionally commenting on what she considered unnecessary exertion of authority by an upperclassman.

We pulled up to the barracks gate only to be directed to unpack there. We then reported to a large room with several tables under letters of the alphabet corresponding to the new cadet's last name. The cadets placed at each table to help were overly polite and highly efficient. As we signed the necessary paperwork, a chill went down my spine. I was transferring all my parental rights to these cadets on the other side of the table.

The last paper signed, the niceties over, "Cadet, say goodbye to your family."

And then, Robert disappeared down a flight of stairs, from which came whining, intermingled with the screaming and yelling of instructions. Could that be the reincarnation of Sgt. Rucker asking, "Are you a prostitute or a fag?

I chuckled aloud.

"What's so funny?"

"Nothing. I was remembering jump school."

An hour later we were in a crowd of parents, craning to capture a glimpse of the new bald cadets in uniform, complete with a duffel bag and a rolled-up mattress. They were being screamed at as if that would mystically maneuver this unformed mass into a predetermined formation. Shortly, the fumbling mob of skinheads was in formation, their backs to the gawking parents.

Comments and calls floated through the crowd of nervous parents and grandparents.

"There he is."

"No, that's not him." The shouting of first names, hoping for a reaction, one followed by "Mommy loves you."

Sure, like a new cadet would answer to that.

The silence of the ride home was only broken by a few sniffles from Carol.

"What are you thinking?" I asked.

She moaned "I can't talk about that now."

We crossed into Pennsylvania before she spoke again, "I guess I'll just have to trust God."

I answered, "Amen"

***

Because of Chuck's courteous and friendly behavior, Mrs. Felice, a neighbor widow lady, landed him his summer job. Her family owned a restaurant and a catering house in Patchogue. His first interview with her son yielded a dishwasher job, followed by the second year working at the clam bar. Chuck's third year he did prep work at a restaurant on the North Shore in Port Jefferson.

Then the King of the Prom loaded his crown and all his summer experience into his new Yugo and headed off to Johnson and Wales University in Providence, Rhode Island, in search of an associate degree in culinary arts. Classes were scheduled Monday through Thursday, which allowed students to work weekends both gaining experience and helping with expenses. After Thursday classes, Chuck would slip into his Yugo and bring home his laundry to his mom. Sometimes he would cook for us, displaying his newfound skills, creating culinary delights not found in the local establishments.

The drive from Providence to Medford was significant but vital. More weekends than not, he would make himself available for weekend work at the Daily News. His persistence caused his name to move to the top of the list, so he worked most weekends and holidays. Each weekend he picked up the paycheck from the previous week, which provided him money for books, knives, and his new girlfriend, Mary.

Graduation day was a joyous family affair. Robert was able to make the trip from Virginia where he was getting ready to report to jump school. I was especially proud that he was following in my footsteps. All in all, the family was thriving and healthy. It was especially comforting to see Carol back to normal. Of course, there was a touch of melancholy because we would not all be together. Robert could wind up stationed anywhere in the world and Chuck had accepted a position at the Sheraton in Lexington, Massachusetts. That, at least, put him near his girl who lived in Scituate. It wasn't long before they were planning their wedding.

***

Life was good. The house was empty, and we were enjoying our newfound freedom. Freedom to roam scantily dressed about the house and display our affections, any time or any place that tickled our fancies.

Eventually, the silence created by the boys' absence drove Carol to find a position with a vitamin company. This added to our discretionary income which we spread among the finer dining establishments in New York. When we weren't eating on Long Island's Gold Coast, the culinary school offered the most excellent cuisine in Providence.

***

One memorable weekend, we met Tracy, Bob's new girlfriend. The romance appeared to be growing more serious and before long we were pleased to meet her parents, sister, and brother-in-law. In time the couple was planning their wedding that would take place following graduation. Robert would be commissioned a second lieutenant and receive orders for the artillery school in Texas. All this happened on his birthday May 15, 1987, the 123rd anniversary of the Battle of New Market. In 1864, The VMI Corps of Cadets was ordered to join Gen. John C Breckenridge and the Confederate forces near Staunton, Virginia. Of the 257 cadets, 10 were killed and 45 were wounded. Despite their losses, they were credited with the victory. After the parade and the anniversary celebration came graduation with all its pomp and circumstance and the mass exodus for summer break.

The Phillips clan could now relax and enjoy the lieutenant's birthday party and his wedding on Sunday. What a weekend! Full of memorable sights; the graduation, the horse-drawn carriage delivering the bride to the church, and the Cadet Honor Guard, in full uniform, sabers drawn, forming the first pathway for the new man and wife.

21. Consider the Newspaper

Consider the newspaper, the physical object. Printed on processed wood pulp, shot upward on rollers at high speed as ink is applied, gathered, folded, and bundled, dropped off at newsstands and bodegas, or delivered to doorsteps.

In 1925, yes 1925, New York City had nineteen daily newspapers with a total circulation exceeding the population of the city. By the end of World War II, half of those papers were gone, but circulation was even higher. By1966, there were only three papers left.

The endless strikes had helped kill off all the News' tabloid rivals, except the Post. The News' once healthy profit margins shrunk rapidly. By the late '60s and early '70s, the News management team questioned whether it made sense to continue to invest in what looked like a dying industry.

In 1978, an 88-day strike cost the Daily News $20 million, 200,000 in Sunday circulation, and 300,000 in daily circulation. The paper continued to bleed financially. The parent company, the Tribune Company of Chicago, offered both the Washington Star publisher, Joseph Allbritton, and the New York real estate developer, Donald Trump, $100 million to take the News off its hands. Both declined.

The Tribune Company, which was preparing an initial public offering of its stock, reported in their 1983 prospectus that: "Due to rising costs and operating inefficiencies, the New York Daily News incurred operating losses of $12.6 million and $14.3 million in 1981 and 82, respectively. After exploring the possibilities of selling the newspaper, the company in April 1982 began a recovery program to return the Daily News to profitability. The first phase of the program was to negotiate with the eleven unions representing the News employees to reduce operating costs. Those negotiations were satisfactorily concluded in October 1982 and resulted in staff reductions, involuntary employment termination, incentives or job buyouts, and work rule changes to the union contracts, which had been scheduled to expire March 1984 were extended through March 1987."

***

On the eve of April Fools Day, 1990 the unions and the Tribune management faced each other in a tense situation that would decide both the future lives of 3000 workers at the Daily News and the future of the newspaper itself. Sitting in for the News management company was Robert Ballow, demanding nothing less than unilateral control over manpower and working conditions at the Daily News.

Ballow was a stocky, six feet, dark-haired, deep-voiced, slow-talking, Tennessean. A newspaper man first, he came to the law in middle age. The choice of Ballow as labor council had a certain inevitability, as one of the news executives put it, for a battle that, by newspaper industry standards, promised to be "the Super Bowl of labor relations."

On the night of October 24, 1990, the confrontation at the Daily News reached its peak. A delivery driver had an injured knee and was counting and inspecting bundles of papers from a sitting position. After months of convincing their members to stay at work despite the absence of a contract, the bum knee of a newspaper delivery driver supplied the spark that ignited the walkout. Accounts differ on what exactly happened that night. Whether the drivers briefly caucused on the job or were locked out by management when they went to check on their fellow drivers is unclear. The regional National Labor Relations Board ruled that the company had locked out the workers. In any case, the Daily News was prepared: Twenty minutes after the drivers left or were forced off their jobs, replacement workers arrived in heavily guarded buses.

By the time the first bus of replacement workers arrived, about 200 union drivers were out on the street, including nearly all that should have been inside and many who would normally be out-side by the loading docks. Police in riot gear dotted the asphalt landscape at the intersections and the entrance to the building. The acid that was lining our stomachs started to bubble like the lava in the belly of a volcano. We were perched in the fourth-floor plate room looking out the windows and waiting for instructions to work or to walk. When the time came, we were ordered, "Take only your personal property and leave the building."

Shortly after midnight, I joined about a hundred strikers and began an informal demonstration, marching from Pacific Street to Sixth Avenue to Atlantic Avenue, chanting, "Don't buy the News." This went on for about an hour when one of the "scab" buses was spotted parked on the corner of Atlantic and Flatbush, with only the driver inside. As the crowd swarmed toward the un-protected target, a striker shouted, "Tip it over." The crowd re-sponded and began rhythmically rocking the bus side to side, each time a little bit closer to flipping it, as the terrified driver scram-bled to find a safe place from which to take the fall. The bus was just about to go when a single riot-equipped police officer showed up and succeeded in chasing the strikers away. The mob of angry strikers, slightly shamed by this setback, consoled themselves by marching back toward the plant and building a bonfire in the street with discarded wooden warehouse pallets.

It was approximately 3 a.m. when the delivery trucks started rolling out and were pelted with rocks and bricks. They were able to get away because a cordon of eighteen police vehicles and riot cops kept strikers from blocking their way. Frank Pepe, a fellow pressman, ran charging into the middle of Atlantic Avenue, be-tween the police escort and the News truck, heaving a cinder block up into the windshield and gracefully spinning around like a matador in a bull fight. The concrete block smashed through the window, but it didn't stop the truck. I stood there breathless. I was certain I would be mopping my friend from the asphalt.

The News' human resources staff began arriving at the 42nd Street headquarters at first light. Their task was to hire hundreds of people in the following days, some of whom would be put to work that very night, and safely transport them into the plants via guarded buses. At that early hour, the building was ringed with police in full riot gear, including helmets and face shields, adding a sci-fi touch to the already surreal sight of Manhattan's concrete canyons at dawn.

The next day, the number of serious attacks on delivery trucks or other Daily News property rose substantially. There were many reports of trucks being run off the road, their papers being stolen while drivers were making a delivery, tires slashed, radiators punctured, windows smashed, and unoccupied trucks burned. Replacement workers, drivers, in particular, began to receive death threats. By Saturday morning there had been more than two dozen arrests for violence. Eight News trucks, worth $35,000 each, had been destroyed by fire and sixty more had sustained significant damage.

Though the advertisers had been unmoved by the prestrike boycott, they fell away quickly as soon as it became clear that the News was losing the battle in the street. Some smaller advertisers cut back or dropped out almost at once. The bedrock department store accounts, Macy's (worth more than $10 million a year), Abraham and Strauss, Alexander's, and others held firm.

Two of the three rival New York newspapers, the Times and News Day, covered the first week's violence thoroughly. The police, through Operation Safe Corridor, did keep the strikers from shutting down the plant and saw the trucks safely off to their routes.

It was the first week of the strike when Union President Jack Kennedy approached me about working in the boycott office. "We need some well-spoken people to call advertisers and convince them to stop or suspend advertising in the News." I joined the small group manning the phones, keeping notes on everyone we spoke to. Some guild workers were feeding us names and numbers of executives. It was important to be courteous and not to make any threats, just in case we were being recorded.

The News' most influential columnist, Mike McAlary, after a few days on the picket line, signed a six-figure contract with the New York Post and maintained his solidarity from within his column. At the labor rally on November 1, in front of the New York Daily News headquarters, Mike told the crowd "We're winning, there's no question, you almost have to be a scuba diver to read the Daily News, because all the papers are under water."

Union presidents from the transportation workers, the Teamsters, and the municipal workers, all proclaimed there would be no peace in town until we win. Several of the union leaders approached Cardinal John O'Connor asking him for moral support for the strikers. After the meeting, he told the press he was convinced the unions "want to operate fairly, to do the right thing." He denounced the notion that the violence added up to anything more than the sporadic outbursts of frustrated individuals.

Frustrated I was, but I continued to do my part by manning the phones. The boycott office became a processing center for information. At first, it was a rumor, then it was verified, Mike Wallace and the Sixty Minutes team would be interviewing union leaders at a particular restaurant in Brooklyn. I saw this as an opportunity to stand with my brothers. There were twelve of us, arranged in a group setting, for the basic question and answer format. Mr. Wallace brought up the name of Bob Ballow.

I spoke up, "He is a serial rapist. "

"Wait a minute, wait, cut, cut. What did you say?"

"He's a rapist." My immediate thought was that I couldn't say that on television.

"What do you mean by that?'

"Rape by any other name is still rape."

"Good, good. We're going to roll this again," he said. "Same question, same answer."

I went on to explain that union-busting is industrial rape and that Ballow was behaving with depraved indifference for anyone but himself. By Sunday evening, I had my TV debut. By

Wednesday, thousands of red bumper stickers were circulating with "Union Busting is Industrial Rape."

Like dominoes, they began to fall. Hillside Bedding, an important midsize account, announced it would get out of the News. On November 10, Alexander's placed 13 pages in the Post, an unheard-of event before the strike. Five days later, on November 15, News America Publishing, a major coupon distributor, said it was no longer using the Sunday News to carry its color coupon inserts, a decision that cost the News $100,000 a week. The next day, Pergament Home Centers, their second-largest account after Macy's, abandoned ship and announced its intention to seek compensation for earlier shortfalls in promised circulation. Finally, on Thursday, November 22nd, the day of the Macy's Thanksgiving Day Parade, an event in which the News had previously announced it would not take part for fear that the union violence might disrupt the festivities, Macy's decided to pull out. A&S and Alexander's soon followed suit. With their withdrawal, the News ceased to function as an advertising vehicle and was losing between $750,000 and $1 million per day. As rich as the Tribune Company was, five to seven million dollars in losses a week was too much. If the company could not get the advertisers back on board, this battle would be lost.

With circulation and ad revenues gone, Ballow's waiting game suddenly turned into a losing proposition. The company's goal became blatantly political: force the mayor, the governor, and the police to track the violence to its source and put a stop to it. The News publisher, Jim Hoge, after months of avoiding the press, began to reemerge to fight for the hearts and minds of New York. It was an uphill battle from the start. Mayor David Dinkins was indebted to organized labor for his victory over Ed Koch in the Democratic primary. Governor Mario Cuomo also relied on union support. But the unions did not need outright governmental support, only their passive acquiescence.

There were conflicting reports about the extent of financial losses. By November 18, the New York Times had reported $3.2 million in estimated police overtime partially due to the deployment of the tactical narcotics teams to supervise picket lines.

Everyone had losses: the big guys in the millions, the storekeepers, newsstand operators, and the News workforce who were living on food stamps and strike benefits.

22. Christmas Day 1990

Our family Christmas celebration was held at Grace's, in Mineola, because her home was large and convenient to most of the extended family. Carol and I had driven in from Medford and the festivities were in full swing when we arrived. Gifts were being opened, there was a wall-to-wall buffet, covered with platters of meats, plates of pasta, salads, and chafing dishes, and a bar set with everything to satisfy one's thirst.

We greeted everyone, making our way around the room "Merry Christmas, to all."

Surveying the room, there on the end of the sofa was Veronica, holding a baby on her lap. "Hi, cuz. It looks good on you."

"No, thanks, he goes home with his mother."

After grazing all the gastronomical delights, I chose to join the group of young nephews around the large kitchen table. Soon, Carol became upset because I was sitting with the kids and seemed to be enjoying their off-color jokes.

"I'm ready to go home," she announced.

"It's early." I squawked.

"I don't care. I want you out of here."

I knew by the tone of her voice that she was about to have an evangelical explosion.

"Okay. Let's go. Say your goodbyes."

By the time we got in the car, I was hotter than a firecracker, with an even shorter fuse. I asked. "What the fuck is the matter with you?"

"You, encouraging the kids to tell dirty jokes... you're supposed to be a good Christian example."

"Well, maybe I haven't been canonized like you."

"I can't continue to be with that kind of man."

"You can't be with me?" I quizzed. "I'm not holy enough for you? What do you want?"

"Maybe we should separate," she said.

"You mean divorce?"

"Yes."

I exploded. After all we had been through, what we had overcome, what we agreed was water under the bridge... Our 25th-anniversary party marking a turning point. Over because of a couple of jokes? That's the joke!

I felt the heat in my face. Of all the things for her to suggest. I felt betrayed. Many times, that thought had crossed my mind, but I wouldn't or couldn't leave because of one reason or another. Because of the kids or because she was sick, because of our income.

She went on. "We can sell the house and split the equity. I'll take the furniture and rent an apartment and I'll need the car."

"Wait a minute," I said. "You've given this a lot of thought."

"Yes, I have. I have wanted this for a while."

I almost swallowed my tongue "A divorce?"

"Yes, we'll stay together until after Chuck's wedding."

Without another thought, I blurted out. "You got it!"

The ride home was silent. I knew both of our minds were working overtime. How much equity did we have in the condo? How much for a lawyer? Where will I live? How much will that cost? Everything I thought of had a dollar sign attached to it. Financially, this was a bad time. I was still on strike and getting a day or two, here and there, at the Times and the Post.

Our short-term living arrangement proved to be awkward. I worked as much as I could and came home late at night or early in the morning, passing like the proverbial ships in the night. I took over paying the bills and gave Carol $200 a week.

One Sunday afternoon, both boys showed up at the house; perhaps planning an intervention.

"You're getting a divorce?"

"Yes" in unison, without hesitation.

"You can't work it out?"

A resounding "No!" from Carol.

They had a few more questions, basically the same ones I had asked myself. The boys didn't know she asked for the divorce, and I didn't think it added anything to the situation, so I said nothing. The boys felt strongly that we should not be living under the same roof.

I agreed to move out as soon as I could, which was the next day. The small four-cylinder Chevy pickup truck had a bench seat, hardly wide enough to serve as a bed until I found a place to live. The truck had a cap over the bed, it was leak-proof and semi-clean. My loose items; underwear, socks, etc. were packed in laundry bags and placed in the bed of the truck with my suit, sports coats, and shirts on hangers laid on top. The last things I packed were my books; Bible commentaries, and two whole semesters of the syllabus. The truck was so tightly packed that if I opened the tailgate, the contents would push out and have to be rearranged.

Driving away from the condo, I had a good feeling about the official separation. There would be no more disagreements, neither openly nor silently, to gnaw at my insides. No more acquiescing to the suggestions made by her parents.

As much as I had grown to love studying, I no longer had a place to do so. My books, lessons, and notes were getting banged around in the truck. When I saw a Baptist church with large grounds, I pulled in and explained my situation to the pastor. He accepted my books and I unloaded them, freeing some space in the truck.

Good news or bad news, depending on your viewpoint, travels fast. My nephew, Eddie, one of the bad boys at the table on

Christmas day, got word to me through his mother that he had room at his house, and I should call him.

It was a short conversation. He gave me the address and directions, I hung up and headed east toward his home in Massapequa.

I had a feeling of Deja Vu as I pulled up to Eddie's house and climbed the five steps to the door.

"Well, here I am."

Patty said, "Come in. Eddie's downstairs cleaning up the bathroom."

"I appreciate you opening your doors to me and I promise I won't be a problem."

Moving day took all of fifteen minutes. The small closet under the stairs was more than enough space for eight or nine things on hangers. The plastic bags with underwear and T-shirts fit well beneath the wrinkled hangings. I placed my traveling alarm click on a small night table next to the high-rise. An extra blanket and pillow had been provided. The last three days and nights I had caught some zzz's either in the truck or on a roll of paper at the Times. The high-rise felt good, and I decided to set the clock and catch a few hours of sleep before the night shift at the Post. I kicked off my shoes and stretched out without disturbing the bedding. That feeling of having been there before came back. It took a few seconds for me to realize this house had the same basic footprint as the house on West End Avenue. How I had enjoyed sitting in that den reminiscing and admiring the wood paneling and how proud I was for having earned, borrowed, and repaid the money to buy that house. Now I was paying rent for a one-room crash pad.

RENT! The mortgage payment and the bills! I had to get the paperwork from Carol, or there would be late charges. The Camry still had payments. We would have to put the condo up for sale. That would be some relief. I searched the white popcorn ceiling for answers, but nothing came. Suddenly, I was drowning in a tidal wave of financial obligation while living on food stamps and strike pay. How did I get into this mess? How could this happen when $60,000 was considered a good income and I had a gross of slightly more than $110,000. Likely, the strike will end, but how and under what terms? Under whose ownership? With what reduced workforce? If the jobs were cut, the outside work at the Post and Times would go to the men with the highest priority, leaving me to "carry a bag." That was a newspaper term for someone who didn't have a steady work situation and went from shop to shop and shift to shift to get a full week's pay or as close to it as possible. I had climbed to the top of this socio-economic ladder with a good income and now I was in a world of hurt.

I honestly don't remember how long after Christmas it was, but I was still living at Eddie's house when I drove over to Mineola to visit Grace. I cautiously approached the rear storm door, greeted by the ferocious Missy the German Shepherd. The dog never allowed a male to enter without a fuss, but a female could enter at any time without even a whimper. I stood at the door until Grace calmed her so that the dog and I could renew our long-standing acquaintance.

We made small talk about her job as a private care nurse. Grace was our go-to person for every sniffle, fever, or cold the kids ever had. Not only medical, but she was a storehouse of motherly wisdom. With seven kids of her own, she had either done it or knew about it, whatever it was.

"I was just going to have a cup of coffee want one?"

"Yes, black please."

The rhythm of the percolator accompanied the aroma of the coffee over the same table that had supported the distasteful jokes of a cluster of young men. I blew the steam from the mug, as Grace said "I saw Veronica the other day. She was shocked to hear about you and Carol. She thought you two would always be together.

"I thought so, too. That's why it took me by surprise. Grace, if it had been a few years ago, it would have been a different story. I thought that was water under the bridge but apparently not. There must have been an undercurrent or some outside influence from someone or something.

She slid the plate of butter cookies in my direction. "Remember Ronnie as a kid? Of course, you do. Claudia and she are the same age."

"Good cookies. I had a nice conversation with her out at Sag Harbor about two years ago. She worked hard to gain her independence and escape the abusive environment at home. Did you know she moved out to St. Louis?" She had shared a few things about her time out there, but I wasn't sure that was to be public knowledge.

Grace topped off my coffee and said, "She's working in Westbury, you know! Days in an accountant's office and nights at Mid-Island Department Store in East Meadow."

Critically, I said, "She's still doing double time?" *I should talk! If I weren't wearing two hats, I wouldn't recognize myself.* "If you see her tell her I said hi."

Grace invited me to stay for dinner, but I was headed out to the picket line.

"Don't get in trouble."

I drove down Jericho Turnpike and headed toward the Cross Island Parkway. When I passed the Knights of Columbus Hall it brought back memories. It was there just 18 months ago, we held my 50th birthday party. It was a kind of childhood reunion. In my mind's eye, I checked off the attendees: Frankie Klinski, the guy who left me at the 106th Precinct because he was only 15; Richie Wilson, Mickey and Josie Menarczyk. Now, that was a love story. Mickey lived in the back apartment over the pizza parlor. He met Josie in the Farrell movie when we were too young to know what love was. Then there was Sue and Georgianna Rouff, two sisters. Sue was younger and a tough kid. Georgianna was more mature and became a police officer on the vice squad. That family lived on 118th Street over the corner butcher shop. The same shop where Dennis Cox started a long career as a meat cutter. Joe Cox was there with Eleanor. By that time, He and Steph were divorced. Steph got tired of waiting and working to rebuild the home and family. Cousin Ronnie was there, too. Georgianna asked me if Ronnie was my wife? Jokingly I said, "No, she's my cousin, but if I wasn't married..." At that point, Ronnie said, "You got to shit or get off the pot." We all laughed.

Thinking of that brought me back to what Grace had said over coffee. I had made it clear there was no chance of reconciliation.

Did that have anything to do with why Grace mentioned Ronnie? Or perhaps Ronnie said something to Grace about me. It didn't matter. It was not the time to pursue a love interest. Lust, however, was another story.

I spent a few hours on the line and with the mob huddled around the warmth of a 55-gallon drum. I listened to sad stories of no money, having to borrow from in-laws, and of a fading romance because of lost income. To that poor fellow, I counseled, "She wasn't right for you if the relationship was based on money." One young fly boy was sitting on a makeshift bench made of two wood top rails from the police barricade perched on two inverted five-gallon paint cans. He removed his work shoes and dropped them into the glowing drum.

"What are you doing?" I asked "

"I'll never need them again."

He slipped into a clean pair of sneakers. Trying to resurrect his spirits, "Don't be so sure! I'll tell you what. I'm going to see those kicks on the press room floor."

He shook his head as he walked away down the cold, dark, dirty Brooklyn street. Inside that barrel, were not only wood scraps and burning boots but the inescapable devastation of hopes and dreams.

***

By March 1991, Robert Maxwell had signed a letter of intent to buy the paper. Assuming he could make satisfactory deals with the union, he would take the News, accepting all assets, liabilities, and obligations, along with a payment from the Tribune Company of 60 million dollars.

Maxwell was a Czechoslovakian-born Jew who had served in the British Army in World War II. By 1950, he had transformed himself into a publishing giant. He growled at the union as he asked for enormous concessions, larger in some ways than what the Tribune Company had asked. But he also flattered them. He agreed to dismiss every replacement worker when he assumed control. He also agreed to dismiss all the non-union supervisors, effectively giving control of the shop floor back to the unions.

***

Traveling into Manhattan on the Long Island Railroad gave me some time to think and prepare for my day. This particular Monday, I did not have much on my schedule. Most of the advertisers had given in to our repeated efforts by phone and street activities.

Our AFL–CIO leader, Margo Hall announced that our budget was rapidly diminishing despite donations from all over the country. She suggested she might no longer be able to cover my train fare. The boycott office had become an auxiliary headquarters for the Allied Printing Trades Council. We did some brainstorming that afternoon and jointly came up with the idea of a fundraising Solidarity Party.

By Thursday afternoon, I had been selected to take the lead in organizing this soiree. Friday was spent searching for a venue large enough to accommodate half the city workers, whom we hoped would buy tickets. Hotels were reluctant to accommodate us, after all the press had not described us as lily-white altar boys.

The Roseland Ballroom in Manhattan rose to the top of the short list of one. It had been a ballroom dance hall and then a disco palace converted from an ice rink. In the 1980s it was considered a dangerous venue, after two fatal shootings and several arrests. But this was the 90s. Despite its reputation, I made an appointment with someone from the Ginsburg family and came up with a plan. The former skating rink had a dance floor of 80 x 200 feet and several bars on the outer ring. Perfect. Monday afternoon I was to return with a $1500 deposit and work out the contract. The union presidents gave me the verbal go-ahead and Monday morning the Garment Workers Union sent the check over by messenger. The whole city was watching and supporting what was going on, knowing that this union-busting cancer could invade their locals. The date was set for Wednesday, March 20th, and plans went ahead at full speed. Bartenders were recruited, volunteers were scheduled, and food was ordered or donated. Bumper stickers, hats, and T-shirts were printed. Union musicians from all over the city volunteered to supply entertainment.

The excitement level was running high and we did our best to disseminate information about the event. We called writers who we knew would show up for a good front-page labor story. By 5 p.m., the working-class crowd started filtering in; transit workers in uniform, men and women in all manner of dress, some with baseball caps depicting their allegiance, pressman with their traditional paper hats, and News employees with Daily News hats and jackets.

During the festivities, word seeped in that a deal was imminent. Soon the word was that they had indeed reached an agreement. I was still somewhat skeptical until I saw Jack Kennedy and George McDonald come through the crowd with Maxwell. I knew then there was good news. Jack said, "We have an announcement to make."

Maxwell smiled broadly as I handed him a glass of champagne and a microphone. Adjusting his blue Daily News hat, he started, "It really was a miracle on 42nd Street. We have a deal!"

I looked at Jack Kennedy, with what must have been disbelief. He gave me his broad Irish smile and the Solidarity Party became a victory celebration.

***

It was with machine precision that our people went back to the press room. The non-union supervisors were conspicuously absent, along with the security guards, dogs, and replacement workers. Everyone was evicted, in the few short hours while we reveled in the bittersweet victory. Those scabs, paid home wreckers and recruited rag-tag opportunists, had packed their bags and disappeared as quickly as they had come on the scene. The page-one story wasn't of the solidarity fundraiser but was instead a large bold headline, "ROLL EM" with Maxwell pictured starting the press. By week's end, the boycott office was closed and everyone went back to work. Margo Hall had enough money left to throw a dinner party for the office staff and a few guests. There were accolades passed around for and by everyone. Over the 147 days, many of us had talked of our impending unemployment. I had mentioned moving to Florida if that happened. Margo had gifts for all of us, the AFL–CIO coffee mug inscribed with "Union Yes" with gold marking around the top and bottom. Twenty-nine years later I still use it almost daily.

Along with my mug came a name and phone number. Margo said, "If you get to Fort Lauderdale call him. Use my name. You'll have a job waiting for you." I have hugged many people, and sometimes it's just routine, but this one was sincere with a true sense of camaraderie. The kind that transcends boundaries and state lines.

Maxwell was able to make a deal in just days that the Tribune Company could not do in two years. Union leaders said it was because he showed them respect, because they believed he wanted the paper to succeed and because, with the News at death's door, they were ready to make a fair deal with almost anyone except the Tribune Company. The total cuts came to 870 jobs. Most of the unions lost at least a third of their total positions. Some did much worse. And those were only the workforce losses. In the coming year, it became clear that the News had lost one-third of its circulation because of the strike.

23. New Beginnings

"Steel and Persampiere. Good morning, how can I help you?"

"Veronica, please."

"This is she."

"Ronnie, it's me, Larry, I'm off the pot."

A pause, a short chuckle, and an apology. "I'm sorry, I didn't mean to laugh but..."

"I know, I thought it was cute to remind you of what you said back in October."

"I don't know whether to say I'm sorry or congratulations."

"Initially, sorry would've been okay, but now – now it's a new beginning."

"In that case, congratulations."

"In that case, let's have a drink."

After some small talk, we agreed to meet at the Piping Rock Restaurant at 5. I pulled into the parking lot about four-thirty. If the caliber of cars was any indication of the clientele, my economy class pick-up brought it down a notch. The spacious lobby was sparkling clean. Passing through the glass doors into the cocktail lounge, the circular bar with its heavy, leather, curved-back stools added to the centrifugal decor. To the right, a raised platform held intimately set tables and chairs intended for drinks rather than dinner. I settled in and was swirling my Remy Martin when she entered. She was backlit by the afternoon sun which outlined her silhouette. The glass doors opened like the curtains at the top of a fashion show runway and she paused a moment for her eyes to adjust. She wore a black business suit accented by a white ruffled blouse and high heels. The sparkling earrings completed the image of a working girl on Manhattan's West side.

I suggested a small table away from the bar with its clinking ice cubes and the noisy three-piece suits. In the flickering candle flame, we reminisced. What unfolded seemed to be years when circumstances, time, and life experience converged to cultivate two individuals now ripe for a new start. The stories were both happy and sad, like the love-hate relationship she had with her father, mostly hate.

After a few cocktails and a light bite, I announced, "As much as I have enjoyed this, I have to get going."

"Ah, work? A necessary evil."

"Especially now. I can drop you at home if you don't mind riding in the truck."

When we arrived at her place, I swiftly ran around and opened the door, offering my hand. As her five-foot-nine-inch frame exited the vehicle, four-inch heels first, her skirt unavoidably rode up, revealing her shapely thighs.

"Thanks for the ride," accompanied by a slight buss on my cheek.

"Thank you for a delightful evening."

That was a cousin kiss. I wondered if she wanted it to be more, too.

Driving down Atlantic Avenue, I kept thinking, *that was not just a catching-up meeting, it was more.* By the time I got to the next light, I convinced myself it wasn't. That ping-pong match went on inside my head until I reached the last traffic light at the News building. By the time I parked the truck on Pacific Street, overlooking the Long Island railroad yard, the ping pong match was a tie. I knew I had to call for a rematch, another cocktail hour encounter.

Three days later I called her. "I had such a good time with you the other night I thought, and stop me if I'm out of line, I thought maybe we could have dinner."

"Maybe we could. And why would that be out of line?"

"I don't know, maybe the cousin thing?

"Let me tell you something. You're much better company than most of the assholes I have had dinner with."

What followed was the first of many dinners and happy hours. We agreed not to advertise it to the family or anyone else.

Piping Rock became our go-to place and in time Mike, the bartender, had either introduced us to or told us about most of his repeat clientele. There was the one who came in off the 5:30 train every day, had one scotch, and waited for his wife to pick him up. Reilly was a stocky man with a bushy mustache, very Irish-looking. I could see him as McNamara, leading the pipes and drums down Fifth Avenue on St. Patrick's Day. He was an immigration lawyer. One of many lawyers who would come in when the Criminal Lawyers Association held their monthly meetings there. Many would also bring their clients in for dinner.

I needed a divorce lawyer and Ronnie suggested her boss's son who had just passed the bar. If he could not help, perhaps he knew someone who could. This first attorney worked out of his apartment in Queens. After several phone calls and letters to Carol's lawyer, my retainer was depleted. Postponement after postponement by her lawyer brought me to the realization that the longer she could put this off, the longer I would be paying her bills plus $800 a month in spending money.

I ended my relationship with the apprentice lawyer, gathered up my records and the history of the unsuccessful arraignments, and went on the hunt for a new attorney; one with some balls.

Bartenders are indeed like psychologists, and they also have great connections. Mike introduced me to Matthew Troy. We established a gin mill relationship and when I told him my story, he recommended his partner.

This guy had a real office with desks and file cabinets, albeit old and refinished. The first visit was enlightening, and after another retainer, I was promised there would be no more postponements. The third time Carol's attorney postponed because his mother-in-law had died, I took a firm stand. I was shocked to receive a summons to appear in court because my attorney was petitioning to be relieved from the case. He wasn't getting anywhere and, apparently, I was a pain in the ass. That is not how it was worded in the court papers, but either way, he won and I was, once again, without a lawyer. Two things I must point out. First, this all happened over about five years, and second, the names have been changed to protect the guilty. They are lawyers you know!

Counselor number three was introduced by "I don't remember" but was highly recommended because of his work in a much-publicized international airline heist at JFK. The receptionist escorted me down a long carpeted bowling alley. At the end, a frosted glass door proclaimed in gold letters Anthony B. Capsule. I thought I had been through the ABCs of this divorce twice already.

I blinked, taking in this tall, Herculean-built suit, thinking he and John Gotti must share the same haberdasher. I eased into the leather chair, with one hand holding the boxy briefcase that once had been my accomplice in transporting stolen beverages from the St. Regis. My other hand passed over the copper upholstery nails. A monster of a grandfather clock glared down, the tick-tocking a vivid reminder that I was being billed by the minute.

"What can I do for you?"

"I've been trying to get a divorce for almost five years."

"Matrimonial law is my specialty."

I had the feeling that if I had said I was charged with murder, that would've been his specialty.

"You are my third attorney." As I started to pass the two files, I leaned forward across the mahogany desk and noted the glass top protecting an Asian hand carving beneath it. Stopping my presentation I exclaimed, "That's a beautiful work of art."

"Thank you, it was a gift from a client following a successful international custody case."

As I slid back into the chair I thought, another specialty. He glanced over the documents, one sheet at a time while I scanned the room. There were framed newspaper headlines that had something to do with his practice. It just so happened I had a few non-collectible "page one" plates from 9/11. It was a double-truck plate (when the photo spans two pages) This one was the front and back page depicting the instant the plane hit the second tower. The photo was etched in the aluminum plate, sure to last forever. *If I offer it to him now, he will think I'm looking for a break. I'll wait until after and make it a gift. That way if he wants to adjust my bill he can.*

He introduced me to an associate, Megan Bradley, saying she was very capable and would take care of everything. I sat at her desk, turned over the files and another retainer fee. What followed were the usual expected letters and calls but we seemed to be making progress. On the morning of our next arraignment, Ronnie came with me.

We stood in the sterile marble corridor outside the court waiting for Megan.

"Here she comes."

"Tell me that's not Megan."

"Yes, that's my lawyer."

"Well, you're never coming here alone again."

"Why, what are you talking about?"

"She's gorgeous."

"You know, I never saw her standing up. She was always behind the desk and she was all business. But you are right, she is gorgeous.

***

In the six years it took to finalize the divorce, my status with the paper changed. Shortly after the strike ended, I was slated to receive my journeyman rating. Oddly enough that meant a cut in pay which I could not refuse. The journeyman/apprentice system was such that the apprentice (boy) did the pre-shift and post-shift grunt work, earning overtime pay on both ends. Big bucks! Through the years, the smaller papers folded, and their employees were absorbed into the surviving ones. Thus, there was an abundance of senior journeymen. By 1967, there were only three papers still actively printing: The Times, The Daily News, and The Post. Advancement came only following a death or retirement.

The candidates for these positions came from a highly scrutinized list. Once you arrived at the top of the list, you were the "top boy" (like it or not). You carry a bag, virtually a migrant employee, toting work clothes, boots, and toiletries from plant to plant until you had a permanent position. That lasted a few months, and then I was back at the News Brooklyn plant where I was comfortable.

This schedule could have played havoc with our fledgling relationship, but we made it work. Sometimes a quick drink and sometimes a romantic dinner ending with a sleepover at Ronnie's apartment.

After a while, the fact that we were an item was no longer a secret. We were becoming involved in each other's day-to-day business. For example, I was extremely grateful for her bookkeeping skills since I had a total lack of or interest in balancing a checkbook. I was content as long as my expenditures did not exceed my balance.

She stepped cautiously into my finances, fully aware of my history with Carol in that regard.

"You are in a financial world of shit!" she warned "It's impossible to keep paying support, lawyers, and living expenses. I want to help."

I was lying across the twin bed, staring at the metal wardrobe closet.

"Did you hear me? I want to help you."

"Yeah, you are helping me. You balanced my checkbook."

"Yes, but did you look at the balance?"

"I know, not much there. Maybe I should try and get a loan from the credit union."

"Then you'll just have another bill to pay. I have an idea. Promise you won't let your pride get in the way."

"What pride? What idea? What are you talking about?"

"I have a savings program at work, set aside for a pension and I can access the funds if I need them."

"No, you can't do that. I appreciate the thought, but you can't screw up your future security."

Taking my hands, she pulled me up to a sitting position. I sat with my legs off the edge of the bed, feet on the floor, and had a flashback of OLPH. "Sit up straight. Put your feet flat on the floor." Now I'm expecting a lecture on finance. Instead, I heard, "When, and it was more than once, I was up against the wall, friends reached out to me. I have never forgotten their kindness. Now it's time for me to help someone get back on their feet.

Hearing it put it that way, a "pay it forward" thing, I agreed. I knew then that sometime in the future, it would be my turn to do the same. With glee, she pushed me back on the bed, climbed on top, and kissed me. She was giddy with excitement, like a child who could not wait to open a present. I had no idea how much we were talking about, but I felt sure it would strengthen our relationship.

We cherished our time together. Just routine life. Trips to the supermarket or coffee at the diner while we waited for the laundromat dryers to do their job. Back at the apartment, folding and untangling the laundry.

"This is yours" as I handed her a pair of lace-trimmed panties.

"Those are yours." Throwing three pairs of formerly white work socks, now ashy colored. Bouncing off me and onto the bed, Ronnie reached over to recover the socks. Being off-balance, I gave her a push and she fell softly onto the clean laundry. Her eyes sent a message of war, I responded with a full-on assault of my own.

There, in a pile of once sorted and folded clothes, I paused to look into those seductive eyes. "This is so much fun."

She allowed her mouth to creep into a grin. Her arms open and extended, she whispered, "Why don't you move in?"

My momentary pause gave cause for her to question.

"Not a good idea?"

"Yes, yes. An exceptionally good idea. I love being here with you and I love you. But you hardly have enough room for yourself."

"It'll be okay. We'll make it work. I just want to wake up with you every morning."

Laundry or no laundry, we celebrated this life-changing decision with afternoon delight.

Monday, I settled up with Eddie and moved to Westbury.

The second floor of the Cape Cod was small, basically a living room-kitchen combination plus a bedroom with an adjoining bath. In today's real estate speak it was an open plan, but you could not plan to do much. We made the best of it. Working nights, I often arrived home with some fresh bialys, making for a pleasant breakfast.

Our arrangement was soon disrupted by a notice of a rent increase. Ronnie felt sure that for the same price we could find something better. She made an appointment to view a one-bedroom at the Fairview Apartments in Mineola. It was a bit rushed because the girl was doing us a favor by showing it during her lunch hour. Walking to the apartment I noticed the absence of any landscape only the smoky gray concrete that framed the blacktop.

The rental agent said, "You work for the Daily News. Do you happen to know Herman Borkhuis?"

"I know Tony Borkhuis, does Herman have a brother?"

"No, that's him. They call him Tony." Suddenly, lunch was not so important to her. Tony, who I knew only casually, was her live-in boyfriend. We took the apartment.

The next time I saw him, I asked, "Hey, Tony, what's with Herman?"

He explained that he was out with the guys one night, trying to pick up some girls. When one of the guys called him Herman, he told them he didn't want to use his real name. He said to call him "Tony," and he'd been Tony ever since. This turned out to be the start of a long, close relationship that saw good times and bad. We worked together, retired together, and moved to Florida together.

***

Ronnie still had a network of friends from her childhood in the Bronx. Many lived on Long Island, and gradually I got to meet them. The Sears family was among them. Too many to remember by name, but they were always a phone call away. One such phone call was made to Tammy when we had to move into the apartment.

"Who is she?"

Ronnie chuckled, "You'll see."

Tammy, a proud former Marine, showed up with a truck, a helper, and enough muscles to make Charles Atlas tremble. At the end of the day, there was no bill. Just a firm handshake and he was gone until the next time.

***

One Saturday, in the spring of 1992, the truck needed an oil change. It was a perfect time to get out of the way while Ronnie was house cleaning. I killed some time by strolling the car lot. A two-seat sports car called my name and I jumped at the opportunity to swap the truck for a vehicle that more closely matched my personality. After all, our relationship was good, my finances in order, and it didn't even occur to me that I needed to discuss such a purchase with Ronnie.

"Honey, honey, come outside. I want to show you something. Look no more truck!"

"You went for an oil change," she said incredulously.

It's been a standing joke now for twenty-plus years, that I can't be trusted to go for an oil change by myself.

***

On the many occasions that Carol and I visited Chuck and Mary, before the 'Christmas Massacre,' I suspected they were co-habiting but kept it to myself. Privately, I told Chuck that I would never show up unannounced. His simple thank you indicated a mutual understanding.

Over the better part of two years, they made their wedding plans, paying for it themselves. Ronnie was invited, but it was not the kind of wedding where you invited your second cousin unless you suspected she was bedding down with dad. The divorce was still in the infant stages, and I thought it smart not to openly acknowledge a relationship for fear that it might come back to bite us.

Our cover story was that we were traveling together for economy's sake. I have no idea whether we were fooling anyone. We did have separate rooms. Where was the economy in that?

The wedding was festive. The bride and groom traveled in a horse-drawn wagon to the reception in a barn. The relaxed atmosphere encouraged dancing on the tables. The next day, my

* 215 *

nephew Louis, proposed to his girl by flying a kite with the tail supporting the words "Will you marry me?" The answer was "yes," and the party started all over again.

The next morning the atmosphere was very cool, to say the least. My good time was apparently too good for Saint Carol. Ronnie and I packed up the sports car and headed north to Boston, a town Ronnie had never seen before.

***

In November 1991, Robert Maxwell died when he fell, jumped, or was pushed off his yacht in the Canary Islands, putting the News in Chapter 11. The new plant was under construction at Liberty Park in Jersey City. I was working less, as a "pressman in charge." I worked nights with my partner, Patty Napoli, and went home every other night. With excess time on my hands, I started looking for a part-time job.

My experience with the small catering business, in addition to Madison Square Garden and IHOP, gave me the confidence to answer an ad for a line cook at the Long Island Yacht Club. I met John Erickson, a Culinary Institute of America grad, who was also the executive chef at the Garden City Country Club. The yacht club was a side gig and soon he entrusted the lunch and dinner meals to Jerry and me.

In due course, John asked me to join the American Culinary Federation (ACF) Long Island Chapter. I did and soon became an executive board member. The chapter's many members were mostly high-end chefs and culinary educators. When it came to kitchen skills, I had little in comparison. What I did have was the ability to organize and socialize which I did with 90 percent of the executive chefs of the better restaurants, clubs, and catering houses.

The ACF was supporting "Share Our Strength," a charity fund-raiser. Our chapter would do the "Taste of Long Island." Who better to do the legwork than someone off several days a week and weekends? I visited restaurants and clubs, pointing out the benefits of exposure and advertising. Each would have a booth offering samples of their signature items. We also solicited wine and liquor distributors, and high-end bakeries that were compet-ing for restaurant business.

This was a challenging and demanding endeavor, but I had a talent for raising donations. I relished the opportunity and soon became obsessed. I had calls to make, meetings to attend, people to meet, other shows to attend, picking brains and pockets wher-ever I could. All this for those less fortunate.

The Huntington Townhouse was a mega bridal factory. After convincing the principals that an event held there would gain them exposure to thousands of people who would otherwise never see the inside of this exquisite establishment, we set the date. Now it was time for printing brochures and tickets.

The event came and went, and I was surprised, proud, and ex-hausted. The final tally totaled $50,000 to feed the hungry. For the first time in my life, I had done something without stealing some for myself. It felt good. As I directed the chefs and vendors to pack up the leftovers for transporting to the soup kitchens, I was reminded of Christ with the loaves and fishes.

24. *Vacation*

One evening at the yacht club, John Erickson asked if I would be interested in going to the Share Our Strength (SOS) Conference in Denver in his place. The hotel and some meals would be covered but I would have to make my travel arrangements.

When I discussed it with Ronnie, she told me our friends Neil and Carmela, were going to Vail at the same time. Given the distance between Vail and Denver, we could make it a vacation. We decided to include a drive through the Rockies and then on to Las Vegas and Los Angeles.

We attended the welcoming cocktail party where we hobnobbing with people from all over the country. Bill Shore, National Chairman of SOS, introduced us to Danny Myers from New York City, Paul Prudhomme from New Orleans, and Jacques Pepin, the world-famous French Chef and Dean of the French Culinary Institute.

The following day and a half consisted of classes and round table discussions on fundraising techniques, both successes and failures. The second afternoon was left open for shopping and sightseeing. With the setting sun casting striped shadows across the mile-high city, we enjoyed a gourmet meal followed by a country-western-themed party that closed out the conference.

During the weekend, we received an invitation from two genuinely nice people; Linda Williams, from a restaurant in Las Vegas, and Juan Gomez from San Diego. They gave us their business cards and we promised to call them when we got into their respective areas.

Vail was breathtaking, both visually and literally. Exiting the car, we at once experienced the thin air. It was difficult to take a deep breath. We were advised that drinking plenty of water would help. We met up with our friends and some of their coworkers for dinner.

With the conference and the one-day visit to Vail in our rear-view mirror, we headed west southwest to Vegas by way of Ouray, Durango, and Four Corners. Ouray is a picturesque town stuck in the 1800s. With a population of one thousand, it was said to have more horses and pack animals than people. Known as the "Switzerland of America," it is situated in a river valley at 8,000 feet, surrounded by the snowcapped San Juan Mountains.

It was on Highway 550, the scenic San Juan Skyway, that I first learned of Ronnie's aversion to high places. Her anxiety became apparent when she discovered the runaway truck ramps. I explained that they were there as a bailout for truck drivers in case their brakes failed. This brought her little comfort. As we traveled through the mountain passes looking over the edges to the valleys below, she continued the trip with one hand on the door and the other one on my thigh, in a death grip. When she saw the sign for the Durango airport, she asked if we could just go home from there. She did not want to continue through the mountains. I studied the map and honestly believed that we had gone through the highest and worst part of the drive. I convinced her that we couldn't get a plane from Durango to New York anyway. My map reading skills left something to be desired, but eventually, the peaks and valleys transitioned into plateaus as we headed toward Four Corners.

From a ski lift in Vail to the scorching sands of The Four Corners Monument, we absorbed the grandeur of this beautiful country. The Four Corners is the only location in the U.S. where four states meet: Colorado, Utah, Arizona, and New Mexico. Most of this area belongs to the Native American nations of the Navajo, Hopi, Ute, and Zuni. In typical tourist style, we photographed each other straddling four states and then picked up some Indian crafts and headed for Las Vegas.

Linda Williams greeted us as we arrived at the Pegasus, an upscale, off-the-strip resort. She was well-versed in Greek mythology and gave us a short dissertation. Pegasus was an immortal winged horse, one of two children of Poseidon and Medusa. He and his brother, Chrysaor, sprang forth from his mother's neck when she was beheaded by Perseus.

According to the myth, Pegasus would create water streams wherever he struck his hoof. At least two famous springs in Greece, both named Hippocrene ("Horse Spring"), were widely believed to have been issued forth in this manner. The more famous one of the two is on Mount Helicon, the sacred abode of the Muses. It's water, when drunk, infused poets with inspiration and creativity.

This talk was a prelude to opening the massive dining room doors. Linda knew the effect that the decor would have on the first-time visitor. The artwork, statuary, crystal chandeliers, and gold leaf trim left us speechless. The dining room was constructed over the Fountain of Muses. The floor was glass, with beautiful tropical fish swimming beneath our feet. We were like two wide-eyed kids on Christmas morning.

We took some time to cruise the Strip. I marveled at the growth since the last time I had driven down the thoroughfare. Back then I was with two women, heading to New York looking for a husband. This time I'm thinking about a new wife.

***

We met Juan Gomez in San Diego. He was of Mexican descent with ties to a poverty pocket south of Tijuana. He invited us to join him on a trip to the Tijuana property, along with his friend, Julio. Ronnie chose to stay behind and see more of San Diego. My new do-good spirit paired with the old adventurous one said "Okay. I'm in."

The crossing was amazingly simple, despite sitting in a long line at the border. Wow, what an eye-opening experience driving through Tijuana. They may have taken me through the worst parts of town, hoping this dude from a life of comparative privilege, might be stimulated to do more with SOS. If that was their intent, it was working. About an hour's drive south of Main Street we ran out of blacktop The further we drove, the worse the roads. Soon it became two dry, clumpy ruts that tossed us side to side in the sun-bleached, body-rotted Chevy SUV.

I'm not too macho to admit that I was just a bit cautious. My military training taught me to observe and to have an exit plan. As I scanned my flanks, no water, no buildings, no electric lines. *Once again, Phillips, you've got more balls than brains.* Just about to ask where we were, about fifty yards ahead, was a cross-road of ruts. Fifty yards further stood four huts, two on each side of the road. This was the local market. The meat was hanging in the open air and fresh, or not so fresh, vegetables lay on a tarp. The other huts presented what appeared to be Goodwill rejects, now available for sale to the still invisible consumer. I was re-lieved when Juan and Julio were recognized by the shopkeepers. Or was that wave just an invitation to purchase? We did not stop. We proceeded down the road and the tension returned. I now had a panoramic view of old junkyard trucks converted to living quar-ters. One small, blue tarp-covered building, without a roof or win-dows, served as a schoolhouse.

Juan was welcomed like the mayor of this little poverty pro-ject. I continued to take in the homeless camp until I realized this was their hometown. God help them. Juan had arranged for us to lunch with the townspeople. I was greeted like a dignitary, and I tried to conceal my shock as I shook hands with everyone, unable to say more than "hola" and "muchas gracias." The ladies covered the makeshift table with an old lace curtain, attempting to cover a hole with a plate.

We were given a tour of the garden which was irrigated with wastewater from the wash trough. The tarps that were spread over the huts to keep them dry also collected their drinking water which was funneled into empty 55-gallon drums. I wondered what had been in those barrels before the drinking water.

My humble silent prayer was for those poor people. Our entree was rice with vegetables grown in the garden. I was grateful the lunch menu did not include meat, having driven past the fly-infested butcher shop. Dessert was a special treat, an enormous zucchini that was infused with sugar and left to dry in the sun. The faded green skin, hard as plastic, was cracked with a machete. The creamy soft pulp stuck to the outer shell. Surprise! It was not half bad.

Back at the hotel, Ronnie reported that she had a delightful day-tour of San Diego and I told her that it was just as well that she had not gone with me. I believed she would have been extremely uncomfortable with the experience. Our return air trip was uneventful.

***

The new News plant construction was progressing and would soon be ready to roll. We received conflicting reports each night. If someone was in or near the new building, they had their take on shape and size. The technology was being reported to be so advanced that we would never get dirty again. Of all the rumors, what scared me the most was the term "computer operated." I had never used a computer, never even typed. I was scared to death.

My anxiety was amplified by asking questions of all the wrong people. Every conversation ended with "Don't worry." In time, some of the information coming into the press room became more accurate and upbeat. "If you want to add impression, hit a button!" Change a margin? No more wrench, just hit a button. To add or adjust color, you do not even leave the console, hit the button. And "don't worry."

It had been about nine months of "don't worry," and like an expectant father you know it's coming, but you don't know when or what it will look like. It will have buttons, so they say. It can feed itself, no pushing rolls of newsprint. It rings a bell when it needs to be changed. Unbelievable!

Patty and I were called into the office to prep for the birth. First, you go to school at the Jersey City plant for two weeks of care and handling training. "Don't worry."

The first day, we walked in with ten other expectant pressmen. They handed me a pad and a pencil. *Oh shit. I have handled C-4, rocket launchers Claymore mines all manner of improvised incendiary devices and I never broke a sweat. But the fear of exposure and embarrassment scared me to death. What happened to "hit a button?"*

School was a combination of classroom and practical application. We got to tickle all those buttons. The downside of this transition to the new plant was travel time and mileage. It would be more than doubled. I presented the dilemma to RonnieShe stood tall and straight in a stylish business suit. With one finger, she stroked her chin.

"Don't worry, we'll move."

"That was a snap decision. You didn't even think about it."

"Yes, I have. The only thing to think about is where we're going to live."

"If you're sure you want to pack up and start over again. We can go apartment hunting this weekend."

"Sounds like a plan."

I was sure of my feelings for her. What may have started as lust had blossomed into a solid love relationship.

***

Union contracts, antiquated equipment, and New York City real estate prices caused the three remaining papers to exit Manhattan. The New York Times found some space in Edison, New Jersey. The Post remained on South Street while their new plant took shape in the Bronx, The News building sparkled in the shadow of Lady Liberty.

The plant relocation sparked some retirements, buyouts, and a reduction in work schedules. Within a few years, almost all the employees found a work situation with which they could live. Tony transferred to the Times Edison plant and he and Carol found an apartment in North Brunswick. Soon we were neighbors. We rented a ground-floor, one-bedroom apartment in the same complex. Having friends close by was a plus. Night shift workers often found it difficult to make acquaintances in a middle-class working community.

The apartment complex was located between two prestigious institutions of higher learning, Princeton and Rutgers. In times past, depending on who I was speaking to, I would say I went to one or the other. Never saying I was enrolled or graduated, just that I went there. I suppose that may have been my conscience reminding me that I short-circuited my education.

The next seven years exposed us to new jobs, people, and opportunities. Ronnie wasted no time and, within a week or so, had found an administrative assistant position with an import-export company.

We became good friends with our next-door neighbors, Denise, Paul, and the mother-in-law. We watched their baby, Brian, grow. On summer nights, we would search for wild rabbits and catch fireflies. Ronnie served a sounding post for Denise.

Weekends were spent strolling arts and craft towns in nearby Pennsylvania where we ventured off to go apple picking. It was a beautiful day. Strolling through the orchard, it was apparent how much we enjoyed our time together. Staring into the trunk of the car, Ronnie turned and said, "What are we going to do with all those f---ing apples?"

"I don't know. I'll think of something."

By the time she got home the next day, I had made seventeen apple pies from scratch. I spent the entire day crafting a variety of different flavors and types. Some were spiked with Kahlua, others with raisins, chocolate, almonds, and various brandies. Acknowledging that we could not eat them all, we shared our wealth with our neighbors.

***

Traditionally, in the press room or more specifically the smoke/break room, someone ran a coffee club. A couple of pressmen would take it upon themselves to supply, brew, clean, and secure the coffee pot in exchange for an honor system donation. The break room was anything but sanitary. The pots were rarely rinsed, much less scoured and the Styrofoam cups always had black fingerprints, even before they were filled.

There was still an abundance of alcohol consumed on the job but coffee was the beverage of choice. It served as a wake-up cup, day or night, as well as a sobering cup before the drive home. It was lucrative and once claimed, the self-appointed proprietors never gave it up.

Patty and I were among the first pressmen in the shiny new plant. The lower level, near the entrance to the building, had a snack bar manned by two or three attendants. Service was slow and it took too long for a quick cup of Joe. We kicked around the idea of starting a coffee club if we could find a table and some-place to secure the pot. I went on a scavenger hunt, found a steel table and a banged-up metal wall locker to secure the supplies, and rolled them down to the break room. The next day, I bought a Mr. Coffee pot and voile! We were in business. Within a month, despite now having three coffee pots, we could not keep up with the demand and the wall locker wasn't large enough.

I met up with the building maintenance man to explain that I needed a large lockable box hung on the wall and the next night we came in to find exactly what I asked for, including hardware but minus a padlock. Now, with a large secure space, we could expand the menu. I had become friendly with the man in the North Brunswick bagel shop and when I tried to buy two dozen bagels at closing time, he refused to charge me because they were going in the garbage anyway. This became a Monday to Friday routine, All we had to do was buy the butter.

Our inventory then expanded to include individually wrapped coffee cakes and other snacks. Responding to a Dunkin' Donuts "going out of business" ad, I purchased a professional coffee maker with five burners and a direct plumbing line for $35. Once again, the maintenance man was at my beck and call and he rigged a copper water line to the new coffee maker. We no longer had daily sales of $40 or $50 but in the hundreds. Saturday and Sunday were zero-dollar days until we found someone to help us out on the weekends.

Rummaging through a garage sale, I found a three-section electric hotplate for five dollars. With that latest edition, we could sell hot dogs with warm buns and sauerkraut.

Once again, our hanging wall store was no longer adequate. We needed more space. I knew I was pushing my luck to ask for more from the big boss. Then it hit me, if we had vending machines, we could also serve the day maintenance people. I found two used vending machines, cheap. After a single weekend, I was flabbergasted by the sales.

I was now shopping the big-box store on Monday afternoon to restock before the crews reported for work. We didn't want anyone to know exactly how much of a moneymaker this was. This venture only required a few hours per week, and we were each making an extra week's pay.

Mr. Dresner, the night supervisor, was aware of our business, and I anticipated that he might attempt a shakedown or try to shut us down. One night he motioned me to the side, and said "Larry, how are you doing with the coffee shop?"

"It's okay, it keeps the men on the floor and out of the snack bar." I was trying to point out the benefit of our existence.

"Let me know if you need anything."

I replied, "Actually there is something. I need a phone. No dial, not for outgoing. It would shorten the downtown when the men are in the break room and are needed on the press. They could just be called instead of someone having to walk across the press room."

The downtime was recorded on every press every night. Extended periods had to be explained. The next night I arrived in the break room to find a shiny red phone on the wall (without a dial).

25. Wakes and Weddings

Grace, the Florence Nightingale of the family, now needed care herself. COPD was the primary cause of her hospitalizations on several occasions. Bob was convinced that he wanted to retire in Florida, and they took several short exploratory trips. The first few years of retirement they would snowbird to a rental apartment in the Fort Lauderdale area. Eventually, they would sell 17 Dow Avenue and buy a lakeside villa in Hobe Sound.

By this time, Marilyn and Ray Cullen, (her second husband), Bob and Grace, Paul, and sister Joan, were all living in Florida. In addition, Claudia and Joe were crashing with Joan during extended vacations. In the summer of 1993, the family converged on the Hollywood, Florida area to attend the wedding of my brother Paul to Lorraine.

It was always a festive occasion when the Phillips clan assembled, and little could dampen the gang's spirits. Not even the supermarket slip-and-fall that broke Paul's leg, only days before the wedding.

When it was suggested they postpone the ceremony, his answer was "No, hell no! Can you set it in a cast? And sit my ass in a wheelchair?" We were not even finished decorating the chair with white crepe paper when we received a call notifying us that

Grace had tripped getting out of the car and broke her pelvis. She was determined to match Paul's strength and tenacity, so we wrapped her walker with matching crepe paper.

Without any further accidents or interruptions, the ceremony went on without a hitch. When it was time for the bride and groom to have their first dance, I quietly asked Lorraine if she wanted me to step in for my brother? She said, "No, hell no!" With a wink and a broad smile, "I'll dance with him and that damn chair." I knew then that Paul had found someone with equal courage and fortitude, and they would make a perfect couple until death do they part.

The trips to Florida had us considering the state through a retirement lens, even though we were still ten to twelve years out. On each visit, we took every opportunity to survey various communities. The west coast became an area of increasing interest and during a Christmas week trip to see the family, we planned a side trip to Tampa after stopping in Hobe Sound to see Grace and Bob.

Christmas greetings were exchanged as we entered the villa. A garland framed the glass doors, highlighting the fully decorated tree, with a pool and lake in the background.

"Nice job, Bob," knowing Grace had little energy to take part in those chores any longer. Grace emerged from the bedroom with her oxygen tube hooked over her ears and the tabs placed on the upper lip forcing the air through her nostrils.

Her face was full and puffy and as I kissed her hello, with labored breathing she asked, "How was your trip?"

"Fine," we replied. Then I asked the dumb question. "How are you doing?"

Her hands went from palms down to palms up and back down with a one-shoulder shrug. I got the impression it was easier to sign than to talk. I was certainly not going to get a thumbs-up any time soon. Annoyed, but grateful for the oxygen generator and the fifty-foot lifeline attached to it. "It's my leech," she quipped. "I can get to the kitchen and the bathroom."

We exchanged Christmas gifts. I opened mine it was a Franklin Mint collectible folding knife with an eagle head sculpture on the hilt. Grace never missed an opportunity to add to my eagle collection. Ronnie's gift was a beautiful, imported crystal vase with a narrow neck; designed for a limited number of flowers so as not to take away from the beauty of the craftsmanship.

Grace was spending most of her waking hours in a chair or bed. Anticipating the drive to Tampa, Ronnie asked, "Do you want us to stay here? We don't have to go. If you need us to do anything, we would be happy to stay."

Grace responded, "Get my brother out of here."

It was always good to renew old friendships in Tampa and enjoy the glistening waters of Tampa Bay. After two days, we returned to Joan's villa in Hollywood to prepare for a New Year's Eve celebration. Looking like a bellhop in shorts, I fumbled through the door. "Hello," but no reply. "Hello?"

Joan emerged from the bedroom, tears slipping from the corners of her eyes, "Grace passed last night". I took refuge in silence. Joan's voice, choked with emotion, "For two, two days she," her voice trailing off "For two days she refused an ambulance. Finally last night she agreed, but it was too late. There was a hint of anger in her speech.

Ronnie, between sobs, said, "She knew what she was doing." I threw her a traitor stare. "That's why she wanted you out of there. That was her dying wish, to spare us the agony of seeing her gasping for air in the final hours. Even in death, she was caring for others."

***

We paid a final tribute to her in her home church in Mineola. I was privileged to remind everyone once more of the greatness of Grace.

"Kahlil Gibran in "The Prophet" speaks of children. 'Your children are not your children. They are sons and daughters of life longing for itself. They come through you but not from you.' Last week, I believe God, in Jesus Christ, reached over and tapped two of heaven's best angels on their shoulders. Jesus was looking over the host of angels looking for the brightest, most beautiful, most gentle, loving, and understanding angels in heaven. I believe they had feet of gold, wings of crystal, and hands as soft as feathers.

As he pulled them close to himself, he said 'Bring my baby home to me.' I believe the message they carried was one of peace, joy, and healing. They must have said, 'Grace, your father in heaven wants to see you. Peace and love await you in the most beautiful mansion.' As her soul and spirit separated from her body, they took on a glow, a brightness equal to that of the Angels as they floated off to heaven."

"Let's leave Grace in her heavenly ascent and come back to earth. I could stand here for a long time talking about all the wonderful memories of Grace. How she gave me my first bicycle before she went into nursing school. How later she asked me to be the godfather of her firstborn. How I called her every time my boys got a runny nose. She was always there for everyone. I am sure we all have our special memories. We all know of her great compassion, in her ability to love without condition. If she had not especially touched each of us, we would not be here today. For all the great things she was and all she has done, we are here, perhaps not to say goodbye but to say thank you."

"Thank you for the bicycle."

"Thank you for clam chowder at Sag Harbor."

"Thank you for almond cookies at Christmas."

"Thank you for getting us through puberty and all the monthly talks late at night."

"Thank you for your encouragement."

"Thank you for courage when I was a wimp."

"Thank you for tuition money."

"Thank you for the parties and the good times, even when you were exhausted."

"Thank you for the endless hours without sleep so we could have the latest fashion sneakers."

"Grace, how could we ever thank you?"

"I remember reading in Proverbs 'Happy is the man/woman who leaves an inheritance for his children's children.' Upon further examination, I realize it was not speaking of money, but of good name and character. How can we thank her except to be like her? Imitation is the best form of flattery. We should ask ourselves, is this the way Grace would have done it? Always have a kind word and keep a good thought. This will make Grace happy in heaven. Grace is on her journey home. She is experiencing a thrill better than a home run, better than the feeling of returning home after a long absence. A thrill more exhilarating than being reunited with loved ones and children."

"When the Yankees won the World Series, they received a ticker-tape parade, with bands and floats, and tons of confetti. How exciting it must have been to be a winner and be honored and praised by the whole city. People by the thousands stood on the street, climbed the light poles and buildings to get a look at the players. They applauded, whistled, yelled, and clapped. They were fans! If we did that in the church here today, we would be fan addicts or fanatics. I don't know about you, but I am fanatical about Grace. I am her best fan! If you are thankful for Grace, if you are one of her fans, then let all that have gone before know, let all the angels in heaven know, Here comes Grace! It is okay to make a joyful noise in church. Celebrate victory over her death."

***

1997. It's a new year, anything but happy. There are few things that bond people more than death and birth. It was no different for Ronnie and me. Shared compassion surfaces when two people feel the same emptiness. There was an insistent, crazy mix of thoughts. Like a brain full of daydreams, they dogged me: getting married and a wedding party without Grace. Ronnie never once mentioned it. We never talked about it. My daydreams followed me into the night. Above the roar of the presses, I continued to juggle these thoughts along with the Sideline Coffee Shop and yeah, even some press room duties.

Then one night, I tried to capture my daydreams on paper. On a roll of newsprint. I started to list random things, some past, some current, some future. When the roll started to move on the conveyor, I quickly tore off the sheet and stuffed it into my vest pocket. That piece of dirty newsprint traveled with me for several weeks, surviving many rewrites and uniform changes.

I had built a portable patio deck of interlocking wood panels. We added a cheap set of outdoor furniture and planted some annuals. It was a sunny spot and it added to our overall comfort. One evening, in July, out on our makeshift deck, Ronnie noticed the ragged piece of newsprint squished inside the pages of a large Father's Day book I had received from Charles.

"What's that?" Ronnie asked.

"Something I wrote. Shall I read it to you?"

ENTER AND LEAVE

From conception and birth,
into school and off to work,
into the service and discharge, too.
Crisis after crisis is all we do.

Life in the 90s, it's no cakewalk.
Economies are bad, crime and violence the talk.
You enter the crisis, time and again,
only to leave and enter again.

The minds so full and busy indeed.
It sends us signals, we often misread.
Our eyes grow dim and hair turns toward white.
Hearts start to fail, a crisis with fright.

Time grows short and we look at our life,
ups and downs and a lot of hype.
Where have we been, what have we done?
Seems like we missed a lot of the fun.

20 plus years with the wife and the kids.
Mortgage, cars, and schools that we did.
We carry an image of what life should be.
Pretending to have, when we're broke as can be.

On you pretend to be this or that.
Now you're wearing someone else's hat.
A cop, a cowboy, a high riding jockey.
Life is nothing less than total mockery.

Where is the peace we've been searching for?
If ever we find it, we always want more.
Is it the house, the car, or the boat?
Struggling so hard to stay afloat.

The peace that I seek is a far better kind.
It's in two hearts when they intertwine.
I found a new lady; my heart just went click!
I've been totally blessed to be with this chick.

The image is gone, no need to pretend.
This magic lady is now my best friend.
Saddles and hats, all washed away.
A new life I've started. I just have to say.

The past is over, all the happy and sad.
The good times I've had and also the bad.
Poverty is still a crisis, for sure,
but with the love we share we're really not poor.

What's lacking in one is found in the other.
Naked our thoughts, two lives without covers.
The end of the crisis, oh yes indeed,
for now, I have all that I need.

"That sounds like a proposal." As happiness bloomed inside her.

"I'm not going down on one knee, but yeah I think it's about time." She agreed, and I felt a renewed burst of energy. The days that followed were full of thoughts, plans, lists, and list revisions and additions; the whos, whats, and what-ifs.

We set a date of October 24th and began our search for a venue. Off we went to Long Island, but The Piping Rock was not equipped for catering. When all inquiries and visits were exhausted, we agreed on The Chateaubriand on Old Country Road in Westbury. They were both reasonable and available. One item remained. Who would officiate?

Ronnie said, "Let's ask the Judge." John Marks, a longtime acquaintance of hers, was a former police officer turned lawyer, and then a Nassau County judge who was affectionately known as "The Judge." Ronnie made the call and he agreed without reservation.

Next was the guest list, invitations and response cards, the bridal party, wedding dress, and music.

Almost a thing of the past, we found an old-fashioned dressmaker with a shop in Highland Park, New Jersey. We made several trips for fittings. Sitting in the waiting room, I heard squeaking on a dry erase board, then scissors cutting fabric. When Ronnie appeared with a bolt of fabric, she whirled around draping the satin cloth in front of her. She was elated with her choices and so was I.

We continued to plod through the rest of the chores, each day checking off another detail. Mid-day coffee on the deck, admiring the late summer blossoms in our garden, I took my coffee mug in both hands and took a sip. *Phillips, you are a fortunate man.* I was so happy for Ronnie. She was excited about the wedding; something she never thought would happen after a life of poverty and abuse.

The coffee break is over. Call Megan Bradley and see if she has a new court date. Because if she doesn't, all our plans will be for naught.

The news was good, we had a date of September 29 at 9:30. "Good. Then it will be final?"

"Unless he gets another postponement."

"Oh no, that can't happen, because if he does, you'll be representing a bigamist. Six years is long enough!"

***

Ronnie took the day off, to join me for the ride to the Nassau County Courthouse. We spotted Megan as we entered the courtroom. The opposing lawyer was with Carol, speaking to the clerk. Tony Capsule, Megan's boss, entered the back of the room and sat on a table that was pushed up against the wall, like Humpty

Dumpty sitting on the wall. He smiled. This gets better. The opposing attorney requested a postponement again, based on having had foot surgery, again! Then he started fake limping toward us.

Seeing Tony, he asked, "What are you doing here?"

"This ends today, not another word."

The postponement was denied, and we were put on the calendar for 1 o'clock

Humpty Dumpty was the nickname for a canon set up on a wall by the Royalists during the English Civil War. After lunch, our Humpty Dumpty cannon let out a roar. It was the final volley, marking the end of my six-year war.

26. The House

The guest list was extensive and we were in agreement on everyone. This was Ronnie's first marriage and we were going to make it as special as we could. And special it was; the meals, the music, and the service. The judge donned his robe and called for everyone's attention.

"Before I start," clearing his throat, "Almost thirty years ago I told Ronnie I was going to marry her. Thank God it's to someone else." When the laughter had settled down, he continued with the service and we were officially man and wife.

Our out-of-town guests stayed at the adjoining Holiday Inn and the party continued in the hallway and any room with the doors open. By midnight it was quiet and all the doors were closed. As we started to loosen our clothes, there came a knock at the door.

"Aunt Ronnie, it's Christopher." We smiled at each other as we welcomed our eight-year-old visitor. Christopher had found out that we paid for his family's trip from North Carolina and despite age, he knew it was proper to thank us in person. We spent some time chatting with this apprentice gentleman and when he had returned to his room, we commented on his maturity and the impression he had left on us. Eight years later, sadly, we attended his funeral, the result of an auto accident. It was the most heavily attended service we had ever seen, a testimony to his popularity and the young adult he had become.

The next morning was breakfast and brief thank yous and goodbyes flying in all directions. The celebration was over and our relationship was officially sealed. Not that it needed any further bonding. I had a feeling of completeness. Whatever life brought our way we would handle it together, just being there for each other, as our parents had been. My mother put up with my father's drinking but proclaimed her love for him until the day she died. Ronnie's mother had tolerated her husband's drink-fueled abuse. I experienced the effects of alcohol as a young adult. I used it to block out overwhelming emotions, or just to bring down the curtain on a bad scene in the jangled playhouse of my mind.

Later in life, I became more accepting of others. I learned to love unconditionally, but it took a lot of introspection, confession, forgiveness, and ongoing spiritual growth. I love the spirit in the man I have become. And I love the woman who has matriculated through life's school of hard knocks, graduating with a master's in both tolerance and compassion.

A year had passed, and we were old married folks; still thinking about a place in Florida. On one of our several visits/house hunting trips, we were directed to a development six miles north of Port Charlotte. Rotunda was a nice golf community, still in the development stages. We entered Rotunda Boulevard, left on Rotunda Circle, and left again to the model homes. It was a mediocre drive, neither one of us was especially excited. We stepped out onto the hot blacktop driveway that ended at the two-car garage. As we entered the model home, our eyes traveled up to the 14-foot cathedral ceiling. As our eyes came back to earth, they focused on the glass living room doors that opened to the lanai, the pool, and the canal just past the sloped lawn.

"Hello," from the man sitting at the kitchen breakfast bar. "I'm Josh. Look around. If you have any questions, I can answer them."

Regaining our composure, *let's not appear too anxious.* First, the two bedrooms with a shared bath, then the family room with four sliding glass doors allowing immediate access to the pool. The kitchen was centrally located between the family area and the formal dining room. The kitchen had a unique alcove with a table and two chairs in an aquarium window. Yes, overlooking the pool. We tried to conceal our giddiness, not wanting to broadcast the fact that we could not afford such a beautiful house and were wasting his time. We strolled across the living room to a pair of ten-foot raised panel, wood double doors. I half expected Loretta Young to throw them open and float into the room in a floor-length negligee. Stepping in, there was a walk-in closet and a king-size bedroom suite. And yes, two more glass doors for access to the pool which apparently could be viewed from every room in the house except the master bathroom. That room had its own water feature, a whirlpool bath large enough for two big people, or four if your skinny and so inclined.

Ronnie encouraged me to move along, but I was curious about the price of this Windex testing laboratory. I settled myself on the barstool next to Josh with all the confidence of a real buyer and asked the price.

"This house is $165,000."

I told him how beautiful it was and that I could not retire for another three years, I thought that was the end of our visit until he said, "Well, why don't you buy the model. I'll lease it back from you and continue to use it. No one will live in it and it will be waiting for you in three years."

Now, my second obstacle, "How much down?

"About 35,000."

"I would have to move some money around and get back to you." Like I had money to move! My next question, "How much would the lease be?"

"How about $1000 a month. I'll write up a sales contract and lease agreement."

Ronnie slid off the barstool. "Let's take another look around."

I had seen enough but was not sure I could trust Josh from 1500 miles away. I would never know what was going on in Rotunda. I would have to raid my 401(k) and half of that would go to Carol when we got the court order.

Josh sensed my hesitancy and offered, "If you are serious and you like this house, I'll pay the entire lease up front after closing, all $36,000."

"So, you'll hold this house for me, you won't sell it out from under me?"

"No."

"You'll do this on a handshake?"

He extended his hand and said, "On my word."

The rest was history. We did it all by mail and eleven hours after the closing, Josh sent me a check by registered mail for $36,000. Effectively, we were homeowners with nothing down.

***

Our conflicting work schedules caused us to draw closer on weekends which were spent making plans for our dream house and eventual retirement. Driving home on a clear autumn morning, I answered a call from Ronnie, "Hi honey what's up? I'll be home shortly."

"A plane flew into the twin towers." Assuming it to be a small plane, I initially passed it off as pilot error or medical emergency. By the time I arrived home, I was informed of the second tower, then the Pentagon. The jet fighters crisscrossing the skies over Manhattan reinforced the thinking that war has come to our shores and had the residual effect of causing everyone to be on edge and living day-to-day in uncertainty Gradually the fury and innuendos transitioned into the sad truth.

***

On April 10, 2002, I received a call from Charles, Carol had passed. Not much was shared about her funeral plans except that, at her request, I was not to attend. I honored her request, but I felt bad that I was not welcome. It always seemed to me that she had regrets about the separation and divorce. She had been a good mother who would walk through fire for her children. She would often go without so the boys could go to sports camp or have the latest equipment. May she rest in peace.

27. Counting the Days

The summer of 2002 was spent shopping for furniture and ne-
cessities to decorate our new home. Fortunoff's Furniture was an
upscale store, originally from Long Island but now with locations
in New Jersey. We meandered through the store, picking up
items.

"What do think of this?"

And then the other, "I like this."

"Oh no, that won't go with anything." This routine continued,
agreeing and disagreeing until we both agreed it was time for a
late lunch or an early dinner. Tomorrow is another day.

"Tomorrow we will look at China and crystal," I smartly
spouted.

She casually replied, "Crystal?"

"Yes, our days of Melmac and jelly glasses are over."

"We don't have any jelly glasses."

Our shopping days continued as I insisted on three types of
wine glasses for when we entertained. It would be first-class; our
flatware was silver with gold accents that matched the gold rims
on the wine glasses. When we set the table, it was stunning, even
when it was only the two of us. Service for 12, plus bed and bath

linens were packed for shipping and started to take over our small apartment.

***

It's a big day, it's a monumental day! After thirty-six years of inhaling ink mist, kerosene, reducer, solvents, and paper dust, my lungs are still functioning without any apparent distress. I'm grateful to God for my considerable good health and pray it continues for many years.

Ronnie and I had diligently planned and packed each parcel for shipping. Josh had vacated the house and had it professionally cleaned. In the bedroom that he used for his office, the carpet had not responded to Stanley Steamers' efforts and replacement was necessary. The house was ready, the moving company was ready, Ronnie and I were so, so ready.

The last night on the job I started with the rounds, saying goodbye to everyone. It was like when the doctor sticks his head in a hospital room and says "Hi, I'm Dr. Phillips and you look good. It's nice to have known you, however many years it was." This was my last night. The only problem was I could not bill them for the visit.

Patty and I agreed to sell the coffee club to two young apprentices. He was not comfortable with sharing the duties with anyone else but me. He was also eyeing retirement in the not-so-distant future. The boys had over ten years in the business and realized the volume that we did. There was no haggling when we set a $20,000 price. The four of us gathered in the smoke room for the ceremonial changing of the guard. We plopped down two sets of keys in exchange for two envelopes with ten large in each. Our ink-stained hands clasped together one last time.

I hesitated on my way through the door, and glanced back at the blue monsters humming and whistling, as thousands of four-color blurred images passed through and over steel rollers, ultimately terminating at the hungry folding rollers. The pounding precautions of the knife blade created the birthing rhythm of the tabloid. One that would be on the street before I left the locker room.

The door closed behind me. Silence is golden. The noise created a tenseness in the body, especially over six to ten hours. That is why the locker room had always been a place of temporary relief. This was my last time to feel that transition to silence. I shuffled toward my locker, noting the ink-stained benches, black grout lines in the tile, and the stainless-steel water fountain that had also turned black. I changed into my street clothes, cautiously ambled to the trashcan, holding my blue work pants, shirt, and shoes high above like a bombardier searching for his target. Bombs away, it felt like the end of thirty-six years of constipation.

***

We arrived in Florida three days before the moving van. We put up in a local motel, spending our days becoming acclimated and shopping for household items. The semi finally pulled up and unloaded 167 items from New Jersey. The furniture from North Carolina followed the next day. By nightfall, we had put most everything in place and collapsed in each other's arms.

The following days we started meeting our neighbors. Tommy and Lisa were from New York, and he was quick to announce that he had once been incarcerated; almost like a badge of honor. Despite that, he seemed to be a nice guy and a good father to his son and daughter.

A few houses to the other side was a very pleasant couple, Jim and Rita from Detroit. They, in turn, introduced us to their friends who were also "snowbirds." These Michiganders were lifelong friends. They were Irish Catholics, for the most part, and had attended Holy Redeemer School. Some had entered the Army together and then returned to work at the Ford Motor Company. It was easy to become comfortable with the union workers who knew all about cars. We were never at a loss for good stories.

Before long I found the Englewood Community Center with an extensive pottery studio where I could further develop my skills on the potter's wheel. Day by day, we built relationships with people of new and varied backgrounds, dwarfing the many newspaper personalities of the past thirty years.

Ronnie had a long-standing friendship with Judy and John whom she had met in St. Louis. Judy had a wallpaper hanging business and John was a long-haul truck driver who, in his spare time, could salvage, dismantle, and reconstruct any car, truck, tractor, or mechanical device. It was no surprise when she offered to do hang the wallpaper on the fourteen-foot wall in the living room. What was a surprise was that they had the entire contents of a former ceramic business, including a kiln. It had been dismantled and transported to Florida in the belly of their motor home. Ceramics is different from pottery, but I made use of the molds, paints, colors, and stains, and tested the kiln. Soon I bought a potter's wheel of my own.

Our ever-expanding circle of friends found us constantly entertaining or being entertained. The annual beach party was held at Englewood Beach on St. Patrick's Day. The local paper headlined it as "senior spring break" with 125 people in attendance and a reported 65 pounds of corned beef.

It was at one of those beach parties I met George Perles. I am not a football fan and didn't even know who he was. He had been Michigan State University head coach for ten years and therefore, immensely popular within the Michigan crowd. He was a pleasure to talk to and took special interest when he heard we were planning to move to a smaller home in nearby North Port. Something with less glass and maintenance.

They had just purchased the same model and when they visited our home, his wife was impressed with our furniture and decor. George latched onto this as a way to avoid taking Sally shopping and handed me his checkbook. "You fill it out. Whatever you want."

I was not comfortable with the whole idea and suggested that perhaps the girls might come up with a fair price since Ronnie knew exactly what we had paid for everything. But he would not take "no" for an answer.

"Here, here, take it. Put a number on it. I don't care." Finally, I did.

They returned to Michigan asking us to arrange to have the furniture trucked over to their new home and have it placed the same way it was in our home. We did so and everyone was happy.

***

We immediately started building another network of friends in North Port. David and Monica Nugent, a young couple with three children, lived two doors away. David worked hard to maintain his contracting business. Jack and Sharon Stawrski lived on the other end of Scarlet Loop. He was semi-retired from a variety of consulting jobs.

Some of the most enjoyable times in North-Port, were with David and Monica's children, showing them how to work with clay and seeing their surprised expressions as their finished items were removed from the kiln.

David made me an offer I couldn't refuse. He built me a studio in my two-car garage for the cost of the material only. Finished in little more than a weekend, I suddenly had a studio within my garage with an entry door and window. Now my garage could be organized so that I had space for my car.

When asked if I was going to the CDD meeting, I was slightly embarrassed. "What's a CDD?"

As it was explained to me, a multi-home development with a commercial section became a CDD or Community Development District, as defined in the Florida statute. I still had no idea what they were talking about but agreed to join my neighbors for the two-hour meeting.

There was a presentation from the board with a Q&A session. Time ran out and the meeting closed with the increased roar of objecting residents falling on deaf ears. The full-time mainte-nance manager was the only one left. I sat in silence, remember-ing my mother's words "If you don't know what you're talking about, keep your mouth shut." However, my eyes and ears were opened wide. I watched Jack ascend to the podium and press for information and answers, pointing out laws and sections of the Florida statutes on the legal operation of a CDD. Jack took verbal potshots at each person on the dais, most of which was referred to the attorney who vowed to get back to him. By the conclusion, not much was resolved, but Jack was a marked man. I was im-pressed with his switch from casual neighbor to well-spoken busi-nessman.

I latched onto Jack to better understand the business of the CDD. We attended a few North Port town hall meetings and I continued to watch him in action. Soon, he was approached to apply for the city manager's position. I was not the only one who was impressed.

The more I learned, the more unhappy I became with the operation of the CDD and the development, in general. North Port was a fertile area for the growing home construction industry and we started looking at some independent builders, like Josh. In short order, we were presenting our financials at the bank. We had selected a custom home with a parcel of land. We quickly modified and redesigned the base model and were choosing colors and pool shapes. Yes, we were well on our way to Florida home number three.

***

Sharon and Jack asked us if we would like to get away for the weekend to a place called The Villages. We all piled into their car and headed north on I75 to exit 329. Passing through Wildwood, I was not impressed. We motored on and things started looking better. "Welcome to the Villages." We were puzzled when we saw The Villages Charter School. Wasn't this a senior community? We all shrugged and continued to the Holiday Inn.

We were all impressed with the landscaping and the absolute absence of any litter, in stark contrast to the compound in North Port. Our first evening found us dancing in the town square to live music, enhanced by an outdoor cocktail bar. Jack and Sharon lit up when the rock 'n roll switched to polka music. They became the lead dancers and I thought we were on an outdoor episode of the Lawrence Welk Show.

Saturday morning, after breakfast, we met with Chris Ludlow, a Village salesman. He spent several hours with us showing us model homes and explaining the hundreds of free amenities. Our second day concluded with dinner and more outdoor dancing. At breakfast on Sunday, I asked Jack if it would be an inconvenience to stay on for one more day. I wanted to call Chris to look for a parcel of land and buy a house. They were agreeable and before the coffee cooled, Chris joined us. The five of us explored the

Villages of Tall Trees and Liberty Park. Liberty Park was, as yet, undeveloped, and only two plots were on hold, giving us our pick of the remaining sites. We chose one across the street from the adult pool, shuffleboard, and horseshoe courts. A closing date was selected, giving us six months to sell and close on the two houses in North Port. Jack, Sharon, and especially Ronnie thought I had lost my mind. For some unknown reason, I moved forward with the utmost confidence.

***

Early in 2005, I developed a pain in my left shoulder. Like most men, I tried to work through it, but it didn't go away. Finally, I saw Dr. Holt in Port Charlotte, x-rays showed nothing, shots did nothing, physical therapy did nothing. I was then referred to the Mayo Clinic in Jacksonville. After completing a series of tests, we met with Dr. Cheshire. He told me that the test showed I had amyotrophic lateral sclerosis.

"Please, doc. Once more in English."

"ALS - Lou Gehrig's disease."

ALS is a progressive motor degenerative disease. It affects nerve cells in the brain and the spinal cord. A-myo-trophic comes from Greek. "A" means no, "myo" refers to muscle, and "trophic" is nourishment. "No muscle nourishment." When a muscle has no nourishment, it atrophies or wastes away. The doctor gave us a booklet that would explain everything. We made a follow-up appointment for six months, to follow the progression.

When we moved to the Villages, I joined an ALS support group that met monthly. I met the other victims of this terrible disease and soon became aware of how fortunate I was by comparison. Mine was not progressing as rapidly as the others.

***

Once we were settled at Liberty Park, I joined the pottery group at the Laurel Manor recreation center. Soon the new recreation center at Lake Miona needed a leader for the pottery club and given that it was closer to Liberty Park, I made myself available.

I learned very quickly that the Villages is the most philanthropic community in the United States, with hundreds of clubs of different types, most of which are involved in raising funds for food banks, soup kitchens, and thrift stores. If there is a need, someone is taking the lead in organizing, equipping, and meeting that need. One of the recipients was the Charter School, in the form of scholarships. The school I had questioned on my first trip to The Villages was for the employees' children.

Many of the residents shared their talents from their former life. Each day we discovered clubs for artists, teachers, nurses, law enforcement, military, etc. Even people who believed they had no talent, developed one.

It wasn't long before I got the bug to do something worthwhile with the new pottery club and I organized an "Empty Bowl" fundraiser. The concept was to make pottery bowls and have a soup supper. The attendees could have a bowl of soup and keep the bowl as a permanent reminder of the hunger in the adjoining towns and the world. The concept was great! The logistics, however, was another story. Who would make the soup? How many bowls could we make? Who would pay for the ingredients? And where would we have the soup supper? Everyone I spoke to was encouraging, as long as they did not have to do the work. I knew the main ingredient was prayer. The prayer was answered "You have not, because you ask not." from James 4:3. And 1st John 5:14 "This is the confidence we have in approaching God: that if we ask anything according to his will, he hears us." So, I asked and was answered. I even had a potter's husband, a lawyer, volunteer to get us tax-exempt with a 501(c)(3) status.

We had the classiest soup supper in the country. The ingredients for the minestrone were donated by the supermarket manager and the tasty soup was prepared by the students under the supervision of Chef John Words, the culinary instructor. Dessert and coffee were provided by Starbucks and entertainment by The Villages cheerleaders. This was the first of several soup suppers that raised over $45,000 in donations. Every dollar going to a worthy cause.

Ronnie had taken up the art of glass fusion. When she requested a meeting room and kiln, she met with opposition stating, "no one knows what that is." She circulated a petition at a craft fair and collected 68 signatures, which she presented to the recreation department. The Villages now has five glass fusion clubs with a waiting list for membership.

***

Between pottery, poetry, fused glass, and fundraising was a visit to the urologist. My elevated PSA of 4.0, top of the acceptable range, was a concern. I was given another pamphlet and told to make a choice: hormones, radiation, or chemo. All of which had possible side effects.

As it happened, Tony Borkhuis, now living in Florida, also had prostate cancer. He had chosen chemo. Brother-in-law Joe Peers' first course of treatment was seed implant. I opted for 42 treatments of closed beam radiation. We all thought, to some degree, our cancer could have been work-related. All of us gave thirty-plus years to the same environment. No matter what treatment you choose, it's temporary and none work the same on everyone. My PSA came down to zero but started to climb again, slowly but steadily until it was once again above 4.0. Tony and Joe have both passed. I keep watching my rising PSA at age 75, but no metastases.

Finally, after multiple visits to Mayo, I was told to go home and die from something else. I was not better but it wasn't progressing fast enough to kill me.

***

You have been following this story in chronological order. The beginning, middle, and the end. As the writer, I tried to chronicle the events and personal history. It is easy to recognize the "once upon a time" beginning. But the middle is more difficult to locate until you find "the happily ever after."

I feel the need to pause to share some up-to-the-minute news that one day will be history. But right now, it has made a searing imprint on my heart. The same heart that loves my wife, my country, and my freedom. The heart that beats with compassion for the more than 300,000 victims of Covid 19, the heart that pumps with pride for medical workers and first responders. It should be recorded that, this author is a veteran, a patriot who salutes the passing colors, who tears up at the playing of the national anthem.

Tears brought on by the survivor's guilt, having prepared for and passed through the Vietnam years unharmed. I have often replied to "Thank you for your service." With "I would do it again." But today, after three days of demonstrations and riots using George Floyd's murder as an excuse to destroy my country state by state, to burn cars, loot stores, and spit at police; those ignorant followers of anarchists need to look into their souls to see that they are destroying the things people worked hard to build. They stole merchandise but most of all, they stole my pride! I sat last night clicking from one news channel to the next, feeling the love of country drain from my being.

To see the American flag flown upside down and painted over with slogans and hate symbols as it waved in front of a looted pharmacy turned my stomach. The symbol of health and wellness is now a smoldering ember of cold-hearted lava brain followers. It steals from me all the goodness I have become in thought and deed.

The inherited prejudice is still pumping through the veins of oh so many people. We need a vaccine more for prejudice than a virus. If only prejudice dialysis, removal of hate with a new infusion of the love, peppered with kindness.

The only thing that helps me, is to turn off the set and pray for those whom God may be about to spit out.

Epilogue

It is the morning of New Year's Eve 2020. I'm slurping my coffee as Ronnie sips her tea. We are reminiscing over how far we have come. Measuring the progress we have made, comparing the small apartments where we grew up in New York City, to the spacious three-bedroom homes we have owned.

"Well, Mr. Phillips, if you will excuse me. I have things to do. You know the house must be clean for the New Year.

"I'm going to sit here and have a second cup." I enjoy reminiscing.

What an enormous life I have been privileged to pass through. Not only wide but long as well. In retrospect, I have rubbed against and rubbed the wrong way a wide spectrum of personalities, many of whom had much to offer. As for me, I think I'm someplace in the midpoint of that spectrum. I look with admiration to those with higher learning and experience. I have shared whatever gifts I have when the opportunity presented itself.

Drifting off into a dreamlike state, I see a cast of characters clicking like an old-fashioned slide show. As I continue through this silent documentary, I see Ozone Park, Fort Dix, and the hills north of San Francisco. The sunlight flickering through the blades of the helicopter as I exit in flight. My firstborn in a fatigue uniform "just like daddy." Unknown then, it would be the first of many, from cadet to colonel. The process continues with an array of "mugshots," with split-second views only long enough to start a thought, and then on to the next. I soon realize those were the people with whom I should have spent more time and kept in touch. For all of those missed opportunities, I am regretful and I apologize.

The clicking continues with images of the priests, ministers, and churches in my life. To Howard Style, David K. Fox, and especially Reverend David Wilkinson, with an open Bible in one hand while broadcasting that reverberating message. "Because you are lukewarm God will spit you out." I will never forget that night at Madison Square Garden and its impact on my life.

Then a transition from snapshots to a smooth, Technicolor film of Ronnie and myself, hand in hand, strolling the Piazza San Marco, the Sistine Chapel, and then to Gaudi's architecture in Barcelona. Enjoying a romantic meal in Sorrento and traversing the stone streets of the old city of Dubrovnik in Croatia. Sailing through the Grand Canal of Venice and sharing the awesome grandeur of the Grand Canyon, the national parks, the Canadian Rockies, and the Gateway Arch to the West...

I was awakened by, "Hey, are you still drinking this coffee?"

"I just went to the movies."

"Really? What did you see?"

"God was showing me the blessings of our life, and you were the leading lady.

Made in the USA
Columbia, SC
05 June 2022

61325920R10146